Partners
in Confederation

Aboriginal Peoples,
Self-Government,
and the
Constitution

Royal Commission
on Aboriginal Peoples

Available in Canada through
your local bookseller
or by mail from
Canada Communication Group – Publishing
Ottawa, Canada K1A 0S9

Canadian Cataloguing in Publication Data

Main entry under title:

Partners in Confederation : aboriginal peoples,
self-government and the Constitution

Cat. no. Z1-1991/1-41-2E
ISBN 0-660-15187-1

1. Native peoples – Canada – Legal status,
laws, etc. 2. Native peoples – Canada –
Politics and government. I. Canada. Royal
Commission on Aboriginal Peoples. II. Title:
Aboriginal peoples, self-government, and the
Constitution.

E92.P37 1993   342.71'0872   C93-099632-1

Issued also in French under the title:
Partenaires au sein de la Confédération.

Canada	Groupe
Communication	Communication
Group	Canada

Publishing   Édition

Contents

Preface

In February 1992, the Royal Commission on Aboriginal Peoples issued a commentary entitled *The Right of Aboriginal Self-Government and the Constitution.* The aim of that commentary was to discuss the then current proposals for constitutional reform as those bore upon the right of Aboriginal peoples to govern themselves. In the commentary we set out a number of criteria to be satisfied by any constitutional provision dealing with the Aboriginal right of self-government; we also reviewed a variety of ways to accommodate that right explicitly in the Constitution.

Since that time the process of constitutional reform has faltered, and the immediate prospects for a further round of negotiations are not bright. However, it is open to question whether constitutional amendment is actually necessary to accommodate the inherent Aboriginal right of self-government. In the present paper the Royal Commission considers the possibility that this right already exists in the Constitution of Canada. The paper discusses the historical and legal grounds for the right and how it might be implemented. At the same time the paper paints a broader and more inclusive picture of the Constitution than that often presented, one that incorporates the perspectives of Aboriginal peoples as well as those of other partners in Confederation. It endeavours to take proper account of the long history of treaties and other relations between Aboriginal peoples and the Crown and to work out the modern implications of the basic principles underpinning those relations. Although the historical portion of this paper focuses particularly on the relationships between Indian First Nations and the Crown, a review of the history of Inuit and Métis as distinct Aboriginal peoples would lead to the same conclusions.

Section 35(1) of the *Constitution Act, 1982* guarantees the existing Aboriginal and treaty rights of the Aboriginal peoples of Canada. As the paper explains, there are persuasive grounds for believing that this provision includes an inherent right of self-government. This view has significant implications for Aboriginal peoples, for federal and provincial governments, and for the public at large. It therefore merits wide public discussion.

The purpose of this paper to trigger such discussion. It is hoped that a review of the grounds on which the constitutional right of self-government can be supported will promote a better understanding of the basic issue and provide a foundation for reasoned dialogue. Our hope is that it will also point the way forward on a question that is important to improved relations between Aboriginal peoples and Canada.

In considering the Aboriginal right of self-government in the Canadian Constitution, Commissioners do not mean to suggest that the Constitution is the only source of this right or that the judicial route is the preferred way to articulate it. Other possible sources for the right exist, such as international law, natural law, treaties, and the laws, constitutions, and spiritual beliefs of Aboriginal peoples; and other methods of articulating the right are available. These topics deserve consideration in their own right. Our aim in this paper, however, is simply to help fill the vacuum left by the failure of the constitutional reform process and to rekindle discussion of the potential for Aboriginal self-government in the existing Constitution.

René Dussault, j.c.a.
Co-Chair

Georges Erasmus
Co-Chair

Introduction

A little over a decade ago, the written Constitution of Canada was amended so as to recognize explicitly the special status and rights of Aboriginal peoples. Section 35 of the *Constitution Act, 1982*[1] recognizes and affirms the existing Aboriginal and treaty rights of the Aboriginal peoples of Canada. The provision covers the Indian, Inuit and Métis peoples and guarantees the rights equally to men and women.

The adoption of this section marked a watershed in relations between Aboriginal peoples and the Canadian state. As the Supreme Court of Canada noted in the *Sparrow* case,[2] decided in 1990,

> ...s. 35(1) of the *Constitution Act, 1982*, represents the culmination of a long and difficult struggle in both the political forum and the courts for the constitutional recognition of aboriginal rights. The strong representations of native associations and other groups concerned with the welfare of Canada's aboriginal peoples made the adoption of s. 35(1) possible...[3]

The Supreme Court observed that the new provision provided a strong constitutional foundation for negotiations between Aboriginal peoples and Canadian governments. The section also afforded Aboriginal peoples protection against certain kinds of legislation. However, in the view of the Court, the significance of section 35 extended beyond these fundamental effects. Quoting from an article by Professor Noel Lyon of Queen's University, it adopted this view:

> ...the context of 1982 is surely enough to tell us that this is not just a codification of the case law on aboriginal rights that had accumulated by 1982. Section 35 calls for a just settlement for aboriginal peoples. It renounces the old rules of the game under which the Crown established courts of law and denied those courts the authority to question sovereign claims made by the Crown.[4]

The Supreme Court stated that, when the purposes of section 35 were taken into account, it was clear that a "generous, liberal interpretation of the words" was demanded.[5] In the Court's view, there was one general guiding principle for understanding section 35, namely:

> The relationship between the Government and aboriginals is trust-like, rather than adversarial, and contemporary recognition and affirmation of aboriginal rights must be defined in light of this historic relationship.[6]

From the time that section 35 was first enacted, observers noted that the right of Aboriginal peoples to govern themselves within Canada was potentially one of the rights recognized in the section. As early as 1983, the report of a Special House of Commons Committee on Indian Self-Government (the Penner Report)[7] observed that the inclusion of Aboriginal and treaty rights in the Constitution may have altered the traditional understanding of governmental powers:

> If, as many assert, the right to self-government exists as an aboriginal right, there could be a substantial re-ordering of powers. Indian governments may have implicit legislative powers that are now unrecognized.[8]

The Penner Report remarked on the fact that many Indian witnesses appearing before the Committee affirmed that the Aboriginal right of self-government had an existing basis in Canadian law. For example, a representative of the Canadian Indian Lawyers' Association, Ms. Judy Sayers, invoked the *Royal Proclamation of 1763* and the *Constitution Act, 1982* and concluded with this statement: "There is in law and history a definite basis for self-determination and self-government."[9]

Noting this possibility, the Penner Committee went on to recommend that the Constitution be amended explicitly to recognize and entrench the right of self-government. Indian governments would then, in the Committee's view, clearly form a distinct order of government in Canada, with their jurisdiction defined.[10]

Over the following decade, the goal of further constitutional reform was actively pursued. Several intensive rounds of constitutional negotiations took place between Aboriginal peoples and the federal and provincial governments.[11] One major aim was to secure explicit constitutional recognition of the right of self-government. These efforts culminated in the detailed Aboriginal amendments proposed in the Charlottetown Accord of 1992.[12] Despite the complexity of these provisions, one simple clause lay at their core; it stated that the Aboriginal peoples of Canada had the inherent right of self-government within Canada.

The demise of the Charlottetown Accord in the fall of 1992 left in its wake a host of unsettled questions. Notwithstanding the unanimity reached during negotiations, the current prospects for constitutional amendments in this area are not favourable. The route of constitutional reform, which seemed promising in the early 1980s, now appears to be blocked temporarily.

As a result, the question held in abeyance over the past decade now resumes its central importance. Is it possible to implement an inherent right of self-government under the current Constitution without the need for constitutional amendment? And is it possible to implement self-government in a manner that satisfies the aspirations and concerns of the various Aboriginal groups, including women's groups, treaty nations, and the national Aboriginal organizations, as well as meeting the needs of federal and provincial governments and the public at large?

In considering these questions, it is helpful to recall exactly what the Charlottetown Accord proposed to do and, more important, what it did *not* propose to do. The draft legal text of October 9, 1992 included the following provision:

> 35.1 (1) The Aboriginal peoples of Canada have the inherent
> right of self-government within Canada.

As the wording indicates, this provision did not claim to create a right of self-government or to grant it to Aboriginal peoples. It affirmed simply that Aboriginal peoples "have" this right, a right described as "inherent". Thus, the draft provision assumed that the right of self-government *already existed* in some sense. The provision was intended merely to confirm the existence of the right and give it explicit constitutional status.

Was the Accord correct in recognizing that the right of self-government already existed in Canadian law? This question is the subject of this paper. In concentrating on Canadian law, we do not mean to rule out other sources for the right of self-government, such as international law, natural law, treaties, or the laws, constitutions, and spiritual beliefs of particular Aboriginal groups. Such sources provide complementary routes to the goal of self-government and a richer and fuller understanding of the right. We hope to explore some of these sources on other occasions. In this paper, however, we focus on the right of self-government in Canadian law, in the belief that this subject provides a good point of departure for the more wide-ranging discussions that need to be pursued.

In the first chapter, we consider the original status of Aboriginal peoples, reviewing their early relations with incoming Europeans, the *Royal Proclamation of 1763*, the doctrine of Aboriginal rights, and the process of building Confederation. Then, in the second chapter, we turn our attention to the effects of the *Constitution Act, 1982*, discussing the status of the inherent right of self-government, the character and scope of that right, and methods of implementing it.

Chapter 1

The Original Status of Aboriginal Peoples

Around the year 1802, a young Quebec lad by the name of William Connolly left his home near Montreal and went west to seek his fortune in the fur trade with the North West Company.[13] A year or so later, William married a young woman of the Cree nation, Suzanne by name. Suzanne was born of a Cree mother and a French-Canadian father and was the step-daughter of a Cree chief at Cumberland House, located west of Lake Winnipeg.[14] The union between William and Suzanne was formed under Cree law by mutual consent, with a gift probably given to Suzanne's step-father. It was never solemnized by a priest or minister. Marriages of this kind were common during that era.

William and Suzanne lived happily together for nearly thirty years and had six children, one of whom later became Lady Amelia Douglas, the wife of the first governor of British Columbia. William Connolly prospered in the fur trade. He was described by a contemporary as "a veritable bon garçon, and an Emeralder of the first order". Upon the merger of the North West Company with the Hudson's Bay Company, Connolly continued on as a chief trader and was later promoted to the position of chief factor.

In 1831, William left the western fur trade and returned to the Montreal area with Suzanne and several of their children. Not long after, however, William decided to treat his first marriage as invalid and married his well-to-do second cousin, Julia Woolrich, in a Catholic ceremony. Suzanne eventually returned west with her younger children and spent her final years living in the Grey

Nuns convent at St. Boniface, where she was supported by William and later Julia. When William died in the late 1840s, he willed all his property to Julia and their two children, cutting Suzanne and her children out of the estate.

Several years after Suzanne's death in 1862, her eldest son, John Connolly, sued Julia Woolrich for a share of his father's estate. This famous case, *Connolly* v. *Woolrich*, was fought through the courts of Quebec and was eventually appealed to the Privy Council in Britain before being settled out of court.[15] The judgements delivered in the case shed a remarkable light on the constitutional status of Aboriginal nations and their relations with incoming French and English settlers.

In support of his claim, John Connolly argued that the marriage between his mother and William Connolly was valid under Cree law and that the couple had been in "community of property", so that each partner to the marriage was entitled to one-half of their jointly owned property. When William died, only his half-share of the property could be left to Julia, with the other half passing automatically to Suzanne as his lawful wife. On Suzanne's death, her children would be entitled to inherit her share of the estate, now in the hands of Julia.

The initial question for the Quebec courts was whether the Cree marriage between Suzanne and William was valid. The lawyer for Julia Woolrich argued that it was not valid. He maintained that English common law was in force in the North West in 1803 and that the union between Suzanne and William did not meet its requirements. Moreover, he said – in an argument that catered to the worst prejudices of the times – the marriage customs of "uncivilized and pagan nations" could not be recognized by the court as validating a marriage, even as between two Native people, much less between a Native and a non-Native.

The Quebec Superior Court rejected Julia Woolrich's arguments. It held that the Cree marriage between Suzanne and William was valid and that their eldest son was entitled to his rightful share of the estate. This decision was maintained on appeal to the Quebec Court of Queen's Bench.

The judgement rendered by Mr. Justice Monk in the Superior Court is particularly interesting and deserves a closer look.[16] Justice Monk stated that he was prepared to assume, for the sake of argument, that the first European traders to inhabit the North West brought with them their own laws as their birthright. Nevertheless, the region was already occupied by "numerous and powerful tribes of Indians; by aboriginal nations, who had been in possession of these countries for ages". Assuming that French or English law had been introduced in the area at some point, "will it be contended that the territorial rights, political organization, such as it was, or the laws and usages of the Indian tribes, were abrogated; that they ceased to exist, when these two European nations began to trade with the aboriginal occupants?" Answering his own question in the negative, Justice Monk wrote: "In my opinion, it is beyond controversy that they did not, that so far from being abolished, they were left in full force, and were not even modified in the slightest degree, in regard to the civil rights of the natives."[17]

Justice Monk supported this conclusion by quoting at length from *Worcester* v. *Georgia*,[18] a landmark case decided in 1832 by the Supreme Court of the United States under Chief Justice Marshall. While the passage quoted is too long to be given in full here, its main ideas are reiterated in the final paragraph. Here Justice Marshall is describing the policy of the British Crown in America before the American Revolution:

> Certain it is, that our history furnishes no example, from the first settlement of our country, *of any attempt on the part of the crown to interfere with the internal affairs of the Indians*, farther than to keep out the agents of foreign powers, who, as traders or otherwise, might seduce them into foreign alliances. The king purchased their lands when they were willing to sell, at a price they were willing to take; but never coerced a surrender of them. *He also purchased their alliance and dependence by subsidies; but never intruded into the interior of their affairs, or interfered with their self-government, so far as respected themselves only.*[19] (emphasis supplied by Justice Monk)

According to this passage, the British Crown did not interfere with the domestic affairs of its Indian allies and dependencies, so that they remained self-governing in internal matters. Adopting this outlook, Justice Monk had no hesitation in holding that "the Indian political and territorial right, laws, and usages remained in full force" in the North West at the relevant time.[20] In summary, then, the decision portrays Aboriginal peoples as autonomous nations living under the protection of the Crown, retaining their territorial rights, political organizations, and common laws.

A number of lessons can be drawn from the *Connolly* v. *Woolrich* case. First, the sources of law and authority in Canada are more diverse than is sometimes assumed. They include the common laws and political systems of Aboriginal nations in addition to the standard range of Euro-Canadian sources. Second, in earlier times, the history of Canada often featured close and relatively harmonious relations between Indigenous peoples and newcomers. The fur trade, which played an important role in the economy of early Canada, was based on long-standing alliances between European fur-traders and Aboriginal hunters and traders. At the personal level, these alliances gave rise to people of mixed origins, who sometimes assimilated into existing groups but in other cases coalesced into distinct social and political communities, as with the Métis of Red River. The third lesson is that, at a certain stage, newcomers have sometimes found it convenient to forget their early alliances and pacts with Indigenous peoples and to construct communities that excluded them and suppressed any local roots. The final lesson is that, despite these efforts, the courts have periodically upheld the original relationship between newcomers and Aboriginal peoples and enforced the rights it embraced. Among these was the right of Aboriginal peoples to conduct their affairs under their own laws, within a larger constitutional framework linking them with the Crown.[21]

The decision in *Connolly* v. *Woolrich* stands in contrast, then, to the common impression that Aboriginal peoples do not have any general right to govern themselves. It is often thought that all governmental authority in Canada flows from the Crown to the federal Parliament and the provincial legislatures, as provided in the Constitution Acts – the basic enactments that form the core of our written Constitution. According to this viewpoint, since the Constitution Acts do not explicitly recognize the existence of Aboriginal governments, the only governmental powers held by Aboriginal peoples are those delegated to them by the federal Parliament or the provincial legislatures, under such statutes as the federal *Indian Act*[22] or the Alberta *Metis Settlements Act*.[23]

This outlook assumes that all law worthy of the name is found in statutes or other written legal instruments. Under this view, if a right has not been enshrined in such a document, it does not amount to a legal right. At best, it is only a moral or political right, which does not have legal status and so cannot be enforced in the ordinary courts. Since the Constitution Acts do not explicitly acknowledge an Aboriginal right of self-government, such a right does not exist as a matter of Canadian law.

However, this viewpoint overlooks important features of our legal system. In reality, the laws of Canada spring from a great variety of sources, both written and unwritten, statutory and customary. It has long been recognized, for example, that the written Constitution is based on fundamental unwritten principles, which govern its status and interpretation.[24] In the province of Quebec, the general laws governing the private affairs of citizens trace their origins in large part to a body of French customary law, the *Coutume de Paris*, which was imported into Canada in the 1600s and embodied in the *Civil Code of Lower Canada* in 1866.[25] In the other provinces, the foundation of the general private law system is English common law, which is a body of unwritten law administered by the courts, with its roots in the Middle Ages.[26] English common law has never been reduced to statutory form, except in partial and fragmentary ways. Over the years, it has become a supple legal instrument, capable of being adapted by the courts to suit changing circumstances and social conditions.

Given the multiple sources of law and rights in Canada, it should come as no surprise that Canadian courts have recognized the existence of a special body of 'Aboriginal rights'. These are based, not on written instruments such as statutes, but on unwritten sources such as long-standing custom and practice. In the *Sparrow* case, for example, the Supreme Court of Canada recognized the

Aboriginal fishing rights of the Musqueam Nation on the basis of evidence "that the Musqueam have lived in the area as an organized society long before the coming of European settlers, and that the taking of salmon was an integral part of their lives and remains so to this day."[27] The Court went on to hold that governmental regulations governing the Musqueam's Aboriginal fishing rights were incapable of delineating the content and scope of the right.[28]

Aboriginal rights include rights to land, rights to hunt and fish, special linguistic, cultural, and religious rights, and rights held under customary systems of Aboriginal law. As we will see, there is good reason to think that they also include rights of self-government. In the words of John Amagoalik, speaking for the Inuit Committee on National Issues in 1983,

> Our position is that aboriginal rights, aboriginal title to land, water and sea ice flow from aboriginal rights; and all rights to practise our customs and traditions, to retain and develop our languages and cultures, and the rights to self-government, all these things flow from the fact that we have aboriginal rights.... In our view, aboriginal rights can also be seen as human rights, because these are the things that we need to continue to survive as distinct peoples in Canada.[29]

This point was echoed by Clem Chartier, speaking on behalf of the Métis National Council:

> What we feel is that aboriginal title or aboriginal right is the right to collective ownership of land, water, resources, both renewable and non-renewable. It is a right to self-government, a right to govern yourselves with your own institutions...[30]

A similar view underlies a resolution passed by the Quebec National Assembly in 1985. This recognizes the existing aboriginal rights of the Indigenous nations of Quebec. It also urges the government of Quebec to conclude with willing Indigenous nations agreements guaranteeing them the exercise of

(a) the right to self-government within Quebec;
(b) the right to their own language, culture and traditions;
(c) the right to own and control land;
(d) the right to hunt, fish, trap, harvest and participate in wildlife management;
(e) the right to participate in, and benefit from, the economic development of Quebec...[31] [translation]

The doctrine of Aboriginal rights is not a modern innovation, invented by courts to remedy injustices perpetrated in the past. It is one of the most ancient and enduring doctrines of Canadian law. It is reflected in the numerous treaties of peace and friendship concluded in the seventeenth and eighteenth centuries between Aboriginal peoples and the French and British Crowns, in the *Royal*

Proclamation of 1763 and other instruments of the same period, in the treaties signed in Ontario, the West, and the North-West during the late nineteenth and early twentieth centuries, in the many statutes dealing with Aboriginal matters from earliest times, and not least in a series of judicial decisions extending over nearly two centuries. It is not possible here to trace the genesis of the doctrine of Aboriginal rights in any detail. However, a few historical snapshots may serve to give some idea of its long and interesting lineage, one with which most Canadians are not familiar.

Early Relations Between Indigenous Americans and Europeans

From the early stages of French settlement, we find harbingers of the doctrine of Aboriginal rights. For example, in 1603 the French Crown issued a Royal Commission to the Sieur de Monts, giving him the authority to represent the King within a huge territory extending along the Atlantic coast from modern New Jersey north to Cape Breton Island and indefinitely westward within the fortieth and forty-sixth parallels.[32] The document makes no attempt to disguise its imperial ambitions: it empowers De Monts to extend the King's authority as far as possible within these limits and to subdue the local inhabitants. Nevertheless, in the same breath, it acknowledges the independent status of the Indigenous peoples of America and recognizes their capacity to conclude treaties of peace and friendship. De Monts is given the following instructions:

> traiter & contracter à même effet paix, alliance & confederation, bonne amitié, correspondance & communication avec lesdits peuples & leurs Princes, ou autres ayans pouvoir & commandement sur eux...

De Monts' Commission portrays treaties as a principal means for enlarging the King's influence in America and mentions the possibility of "confederation" with the Aboriginal peoples. De Monts is told to uphold and observe such treaties scrupulously, provided the Indigenous peoples and their rulers do likewise. If they default on their treaty obligations, De Monts is authorized to resort to war in order to gain at least enough authority among the Indigenous peoples to enable the French to settle in their vicinity and trade with them in peace and security.

Conspicuous in the Commission is the theme of colonization in the service of trade, a theme that featured prominently in France's efforts in Canada and goes some way toward explaining the particular nature of its relations with Aboriginal nations.[33] A flourishing commerce in furs depended on close links with these nations, to the exclusion of rival trading powers such as the Dutch and the English. It also depended on Aboriginal peoples remaining in possession of their territories as their hunting and trapping grounds. Antagonizing Aboriginal groups would deflect the fur trade to Dutch and English entrepots further south; driving them from their lands (assuming this was even possible) would shut down the trade altogether.

The character of French-Aboriginal relations is further illustrated by a peace treaty concluded at Quebec on December 13, 1665.[34] The parties were the representatives of four Iroquois nations (the Onondagas, Cayugas, Senecas, and Oneidas) and the French Crown, as represented by the Seigneur de Tracy, the King's Lieutenant-General in North and South America. Treaty documents of this kind have to be read with caution, because they were usually drafted by the European parties and translated into Aboriginal languages only later, with doubtful accuracy.[35] The text of the treaty of 1665 is heavily coloured by French attitudes and ambitions. However, it is interesting for the light it casts on French perceptions of their relations with Aboriginal peoples.

The text begins by reciting that former French kings had, at some trouble and expense, sent people to discover new countries inhabited by "Nations Sauvages". However, these enterprises had been so unsuccessful that until recently the King's Arms had been carried inland only as far as the island of Montreal. Nevertheless, during the current regime, the road to the Iroquois countries had been opened, and Frenchmen had been sent there "tant pour y establir le nom de Christ, que pour y assujettir à la domination Françoise les Peuples Sauvages qui les habitent". The aim of the present treaty, observes the text, was not to establish a new peace but merely to confirm an existing one, whereby the Iroquois nations would continue to receive the same protection they had previously received from the French Crown.

In the first article of the treaty, the parties forgive each other for any past offences, including those committed against the Iroquois by the Hurons or the Algonquins. The text goes on to stipulate that the Hurons and Algonquins shall not in future be disturbed in their hunting by the Iroquois nations or harassed when travelling to trade with the French, "Ledit Seigneur Roy declarant dés à present qu'il les tient tous, non seulement sous sa Protection, mais comme ses propres Sujets, s'estans une fois donnez à Sa Majesté à titre de sujettion & vasselage".[36] Hostilities between the Iroquois and the Hurons and Algonquins shall cease and the nations shall live in mutual friendship and assistance "sous la protection dudit Seigneur Roy". Overall, these provisions paint the picture of a number of distinct Aboriginal nations living at peace under the suzerainty of the French Crown, each within its own territory.

The territorial and governmental rights of the Aboriginal parties are acknowledged in later articles. The French Crown undertakes to send some French families among the Iroquois nations "pour s'habituer dans leur Païs", on condition that the Iroquois give the French suitable lands for building cabins and planting corn and also extend to the French families communal rights of hunting and fishing. In return, the Iroquois nations agree to send two families each to Montreal, Trois Rivières and Quebec City, where they would be given fields and corn and the privilege of hunting and fishing in common. These provisions acknowledge the Iroquois title to their territories and recognize their power to grant (or not to grant) lands and hunting rights to incoming French settlers. The reciprocal nature of the articles is revealing. It undercuts the exaggerated claims of the French Crown in earlier articles and places them in a more realistic context. Overall, the treaty portrays Aboriginal nations as autonomous, self-governing nations in possession of their territories, within an asserted framework of French suzerainty and protection.

Of course, Aboriginal nations viewed their relations with the French from a different perspective. While outlooks varied from nation to nation, as a rule Aboriginal peoples tended to characterize these relations more in terms of friendship and alliance and less in terms of suzerainty or protection. So, for example, when the British tried to persuade the Micmac to swear allegiance to the British Crown after the French cession of Acadia in 1715, the Micmac replied that the French Crown could not have ceded away their rights since they had always been independent peoples, allies and brothers of the French.[37] Likewise, in 1752 the Abenakis pointedly informed a representative of the Governor at Boston:

> We are entirely free; we are allies of the King of France, from whom we have received the Faith and all sorts of assistance in our necessities; we love that Monarch, and we are strongly attached to his interests.[38]

Nevertheless, the reality of Aboriginal-European relations at this period was remarkably complex and fluid and harboured a great deal more ambiguity than either side was ordinarily inclined to admit.[39] While the French wished to assert some form of suzerainty over neighbouring Aboriginal peoples, in practice they often had to settle for alliances or simple neutrality. And while Indigenous nations sometimes wished to assert their total independence of the French colony, in practice they often found themselves reliant on French trade and protection and increasingly overshadowed by European armed might.

In general, however, the observations of Justice Monk in *Connolly* v. *Woolrich* do not seem too far off the mark. Speaking of the impact of French settlers and trading companies on Aboriginal peoples, he concludes:

> The enterprise and trading operations of these companies and the French colonists generally extended over vast regions of the northern and western portions of this continent. They entered into treaties with the Indian tribes and nations, and carried on a lucrative and extensive fur trade with the natives. Neither the French Government, nor any of its colonists or their trading

> associations, ever attempted, during an intercourse of over two hundred years, to subvert or modify the laws and usages of the aboriginal tribes, except where they had established colonies and permanent settlements, and, then only by persuasion...[40]

The French policy of cultivating the friendship and alliance of Aboriginal peoples was replicated, with somewhat less success, by the burgeoning British colonies to the south.[41] These colonies would have preferred to be in a position to dominate and control their Aboriginal neighbours. However, in practice they were usually reduced to soliciting them as partners in the fur trade and as allies in the struggles with France. So, as with the French, treaties were a common and important feature of British relations with Indigenous American peoples and were usually concluded in accordance with an adapted form of Aboriginal ceremonial.

There was one important difference between British and French practice in this context. The French colony was planted along the shores of the St. Lawrence River, in areas without a strong initial Aboriginal presence, and the colony remained relatively small in numbers.[42] As a result, there was relatively little need for the French to secure lands from their Aboriginal neighbours. By contrast, from an early period, the British colonists found themselves in direct competition with Indigenous people for lands.[43] In the opening stages of settlement, this collision of interests often resulted in warfare and led to the forcible dispossession of Aboriginal nations.[44] Over time, however, a policy developed whereby lands required for settlement would be secured from Aboriginal owners by formal agreement,[45] and treaties involving land cessions soon became a common feature of British-Aboriginal relations. On the other hand, treaties of cession remained a relative rarity among the French. This did not necessarily mean that the French were less willing than the British to acknowledge Aboriginal rights to their territories.[46]

Relations between the British colonies and Aboriginal peoples were complex and diverse, with elements of contradiction and paradox. Nevertheless, by the year 1763, when New France was ceded to the British Crown in the Treaty of Paris, Aboriginal-English relations had stabilized to the point that they could be seen to be grounded in two fundamental principles.

Under the first principle, Aboriginal peoples were generally recognized as autonomous political units capable of holding treaty relations with the Crown. Evidence of this principle can be seen at an early stage of British settlement. It is reflected, for example, in the Royal Charter granted in 1621 to Sir William Alexander for the barony of Nova Scotia. Despite its ethnocentric language, common at this period, the Charter accepts Indigenous Americans as independent peoples with the capacity to conclude treaties. The British King instructs his subjects to "cultivate peace and quiet with the native inhabitants" and gives Alexander the power of arranging and securing peace, alliance, friendship, mutual conferences, assistance, and intercourse with those savage aborigines and their chiefs, and any others bearing rule and power among them; and of preserving and fostering such relations and treaties as they or their aforesaids shall form with them; provided those treaties are, on the other side, kept faithfully by these barbarians; and, unless this be done, of taking up arms against them, whereby they may be reduced to order...[47]

We see further evidence of the same principle in the Royal Instructions sent to the Governor of Nova Scotia a century later, in 1719:

And whereas we have judged it highly necessary for our service that you should cultivate and maintain a strict friendship and good correspondence with the Indians inhabiting within our said province of Nova Scotia, that they may be induced by degrees not only to be good neighbors to our subjects but likewise themselves to become good subjects to us; we do therefore direct you upon your arrival in Nova Scotia to send for the several heads of the said Indian nations or clans and promise them friendship and protection in his Majesty's part; you will likewise bestow upon them in our name as your discretion shall direct such presents as you shall carry from hence for their use.[48]

This provision remained in force with minor variations until at least the 1770s. It recognizes the autonomous status of Indian peoples, organized in "nations" or "clans", with their own leaders. It instructs the Governor to enter into relations with Indian nations with a view to cultivating their friendship; in so doing, it envisages that treaties will be negotiated. This inference is spelled out in revised instructions sent to the Governor in 1749, which directed him explicitly to enter into a treaty with the Indians, promising them the Crown's friendship and protection.[49]

A second principle emerged from British practice. It acknowledged that Aboriginal nations were entitled to the territories in their possession unless or until they ceded them away. The proposition was articulated, for example, by Royal Commissioners appointed by the Crown in 1664 to visit the New England colonies, with the power, among other things, to hear Indian complaints of ill-treatment.[50] One of the matters singled out for criticism by the Commissioners was a Massachusetts law providing that the Indians had a just right to any lands within the colony that they possessed, so long as they had improved these lands "by subduing the same".[51] The law cited several biblical passages in support, in particular Genesis 1:28 and 9:1 and Psalm 115:16. This law, despite its provident appearance, suggested that Indian title would be recognized only over lands that had actually been cultivated or otherwise "improved". Under this criterion, the traditional hunting and fishing grounds of Indian peoples would not have qualified for protection.

The Royal Commissioners censured this provision, commenting that it implied that the Indians "were dispossessed of their land by Scripture, which is both against the honor of God & the justice of the king." They also engaged in some biblical exegesis of their own. Reviewing the famous command to subdue the earth, found in Genesis 1:28, they commented in effect that the term "subdue" should be understood as referring to the establishment of dominion, rather than as laying down a requirement of agriculture. Turning to Psalm 115:16, which states that "the earth hath he given to the children of men", the Commissioners noted somewhat tartly that the phrase "children of men" included Indians as well as English. In conclusion, they reaffirmed the title of Indian peoples to all their lands, both "improved" and "unimproved", stating broadly that "no doubt the country is theirs till they give it or sell it, though it be not improved."[52]

The *Royal Proclamation of 1763*

When New France was ceded to the British Crown in 1763, the British were confronted with the twin problems of winning the friendship and trust of France's former Indian allies and dealing with the mounting dissatisfaction of its own Indian allies.[53] The basic thrust of British policy is indicated in an official despatch sent in January 1763 by Lord Egremont, Secretary of State for the Southern Department, to Sir Jeffrey Amherst, Commander in Chief of the British forces in America. Referring to the danger of an Indian war, Egremont states that the King wished

> to conciliate the Affection of the Indian Nations, by every Act of strict Justice, and by affording them His Royal Protection from any Incroachment on the Lands they have reserved to themselves, for their hunting Grounds, & for their own Support & Habitation.[54]

Egremont also informs Amherst that a plan to secure this objective is currently under consideration.

A few months later, Egremont sent a circular letter to the Superintendent for the Southern Indians and to several colonial governors, drawing their attention to the fact that the departure of the French and the Spanish from the region would undoubtedly alarm the Indians. Egremont advises that it is necessary to gain the confidence and good will of the Indians and to dispel the false idea that the English "entertain a settled Design of extirpating the whole Indian Race, with a View to possess & enjoy their Lands". With this goal in mind, Egremont orders the officials to summon a meeting with the chiefs of all the major southern tribes, so as to make Britain's good intentions clear and to promise "a continual Attention to their Interests, & ...a Readiness upon all Occasions to do them Justice."[55]

These concerns were reinforced by the outbreak of the famous Indian war, called Pontiac's War, which swept through the American interior in the summer of 1763. In the end, the British government decided to issue a Royal Proclamation publicly declaring its fundamental policies toward the Indian nations and making arrangements for the territories recently ceded by France and Spain.[56] This Proclamation, which was issued on October 7, 1763, has been characterized by Justice Hall of the Supreme Court of Canada as an executive order having the force of an act of Parliament and as the Indian Bill of Rights. "Its force as a statute," he comments, "is analogous to the status of *Magna Carta* which has always been considered to be the law throughout the Empire. It was a law which followed the flag as England assumed jurisdiction over newly-discovered or acquired lands or territories."[57]

The *Proclamation of 1763* is a complex document, with several distinct parts and numerous subdivisions. We should be wary of attempts to sum it up in a single phrase. One major part of the Proclamation is devoted to Indian nations; another lays down the basic constitution for Quebec and several other new colonies; another part deals with colonial boundaries. As we will see, this structural complexity is fundamental to the Proclamation and indeed to the constitutional framework of British North America as a whole.

The overall perspective informing the part of the Proclamation devoted to Indian nations is captured in an introductory preamble:

> And whereas it is just and reasonable, and essential to Our Interest and the Security of Our Colonies, that the several Nations or Tribes of Indians, with whom We are connected, and who live under Our Protection, should not be molested or disturbed in the Possession of such Parts of Our Dominions and Territories as, not having been ceded to, or purchased by Us, are reserved to them, or any of them, as their Hunting Grounds...[58]

This passage portrays Indian nations as autonomous political units living under the Crown's protection and retaining their internal political authority and their territories. These territories should not be granted or appropriated without Indian consent. The preamble thus incorporates the two basic principles of British-Indian relations identified earlier, principles that were consistent with the practice of the French Crown.

The mixture of strategic and equitable considerations that gave rise to the Proclamation is reflected in a later passage. The King refers to the "great Frauds and Abuses" committed in the past by individuals purchasing lands from the Indians, "to the great Prejudice of Our Interests, and to the great Dissatisfaction of the said Indians". He goes on to express his determination to prevent such irregularities in the future "to the End that the Indians may be convinced of Our Justice, and determined Resolution to remove all reasonable Cause of

Discontent". To implement this policy, the King forbids private individuals to purchase any lands from the Indians. He also lays down a procedure governing the voluntary cession of Indian lands to the Crown:

> if, at any Time, any of the said Indians should be inclined to dispose of the said Lands, the same shall be purchased only for Us, in Our Name, at some publick Meeting or Assembly of the said Indians to be held for that Purpose by the Governor or Commander in Chief of Our Colonies respectively, within which they shall lie...

As with the preamble, this passage envisages the existence of self-contained Indian nations, which hold their lands under British protection and maintain relations with the Crown. When a nation is disposed to transfer any of its lands to the Crown, it should meet in assembly to deal with the governor or commander in chief of the colony concerned. The land transfer is effected by mutual agreement or treaty. The passage presupposes that each Indian nation has an internal political structure that enables binding decisions to be taken in assembly. However, the Proclamation does not lay down the precise procedure to be followed or the degree of consent required, presumedly leaving that to be governed by the law of the Aboriginal nation concerned or to the inter-societal practice developed in the course of British-Aboriginal relations.

In summary, the Proclamation portrays Aboriginal nations as autonomous political units living under the Crown's protection, holding inherent authority over their internal affairs and the power to deal with the Crown by way of treaty and agreement. It views the links between Aboriginal peoples and the Crown as broadly "confederal".

Relations between the Crown and Aboriginal peoples differed from those between the Crown and its settler colonies. This difference is reflected in the structure of the Proclamation. In a separate part, it deals with constitutional arrangements in Quebec and three other new colonies.[59] This part opens with a preamble:

> And whereas it will greatly contribute to the speedy settling Our said new Governments, that Our loving Subjects should be informed of Our Paternal Care for the Security of the Liberties and Properties of those who are and shall become Inhabitants thereof...

To this end, the King directs the colonial governors to summon representative assemblies as soon as circumstances permit. The governors are given the power, together with their councils and assemblies, to make laws "for the Publick Peace, Welfare, and Good Government" of the colonies. The latter phrase (or some variation on it) was a standard feature of colonial grants and, in the absence of qualifying words, was understood to confer broad legislative powers.[60]

The Proclamation goes on to provide that, in the meantime and until representative assemblies can be called, the inhabitants of the colonies "may confide in Our Royal Protection for the Enjoyment of the Benefit of the Laws of Our Realm of England". For this purpose, the governors are authorized to set up courts of public justice "for the hearing and determining all Causes, as well Criminal as Civil, according to Law and Equity, and as near as may be agreeable to the Laws of England".

These provisions established the basic constitutional framework of Quebec. They did not interfere with the separate provisions dealing with Indian nations. To the contrary, the segmented structure of the Proclamation reflected the established practice, under which Aboriginal nations were treated as distinct entities, with internal constitutions and laws differing from those of the settler colonies and holding particular relations with the Crown through its local representatives.

This state of affairs is reflected in Royal Instructions sent to the Governor of Quebec a few months later, in December 1763.[61] The King states:

> And whereas Our Province of Quebec is in part inhabited and possessed by several Nations and Tribes of Indians, with whom it is both necessary and expedient to cultivate and maintain a strict Friendship and good Correspondence, so that they may be induced by Degrees, not only to be good Neighbours to Our Subjects, but likewise themselves to become good Subjects to Us; You are therefore, as soon as you conveniently can, to appoint a proper Person or Persons to assemble, and treat with the said Indians, promising and assuring them of Protection and Friendship on Our part, and delivering them such Presents, as shall be sent to you for that purpose.[62]

The King directs the Governor to gather information about these bodies of Indians, "of the manner of their Lives, and the Rules and Constitutions, by which they are governed or regulated", thus recognizing their particular governmental structures and laws. The Instructions go on to state: "And You are upon no Account to molest or disturb them in the Possession of such Parts of the said Province, as they at present occupy or possess".[63] The text explicitly links this directive to the Royal Proclamation, stating:

> Whereas We have, by Our Proclamation..., strictly forbid, on pain of Our Displeasure, all Our Subjects from making any Purchases or Settlements whatever, or taking Possession of any of the Lands reserved to the several Nations of Indians, with whom We are connected, and who live under Our Protection, without Our especial Leave for that Purpose first obtained; It is Our express Will and Pleasure, that you take the most effectual

> Care that Our Royal Directions herein be punctually complied
> with...[64]

There was a basic difference between the constitutions of Aboriginal nations protected by the Crown and the constitutions of the settler colonies. The latter stemmed largely (if not entirely) from explicit grants, in the form of royal charters, proclamations, commissions, instructions, or acts of Parliament, as supplemented by basic unwritten principles. By contrast, the Aboriginal constitutions sprang from within and were nourished by the inherent powers of the nations concerned. These powers were modified over time by relations with the Crown and by certain customary principles generated by Aboriginal-Crown practice. Nevertheless, through all these changes, Aboriginal constitutions retained their original roots within the communities concerned.

The vision embodied in the *Royal Proclamation of 1763* was coloured by the imperial ambitions of Great Britain, which was seeking to extend its influence and control in North America. Nevertheless, when seen in another light, it has certain points of correspondence with the traditional Iroquois image of the Tree of Peace, as expressed for example by the Onondaga sachem, Sadeganaktie, during negotiations with the English at the city of Albany in 1698:

> ...all of us sit under the shadow of that great Tree, which is full
> of Leaves, and whose roots and branches extend not only to the
> Places and Houses where we reside, but also to the utmost limits of our great King's dominion of this Continent of America,
> which Tree is now become a Tree of Welfare and Peace, and
> our living under it for the time to come will make us enjoy more
> ease, and live with greater advantage than we have done for several years past.[65]

The Doctrine of Aboriginal Rights

The principles animating the decision in *Connolly* v. *Woolrich* form the core of the modern Canadian law of Aboriginal rights.[66] This body of law defines the basic constitutional links between Aboriginal peoples and the Crown and regulates the interaction between general Canadian systems of law and government on the one hand and Aboriginal laws, governmental institutions, and territories on the other. It states the presumptive terms under which Aboriginal nations entered into confederal relationships with the Crown – terms that, in a modified form, continue to govern their links with the Canadian Crown today.[67]

In a series of landmark decisions delivered over the past two decades, the Supreme Court of Canada has upheld the view that Aboriginal rights exist under Canadian law and are entitled to judicial recognition throughout Canada.[68] As Justice Judson stated in the *Calder* case:

> ...the fact is that when the settlers came, the Indians were there, organized in societies and occupying the land as their forefathers had done for centuries. This is what Indian title means...[69]

Speaking for a unanimous Supreme Court in *Roberts* v. *Canada* (1989), Justice Bertha Wilson held that the law of Aboriginal title is "federal common law", that is, a body of unwritten law operating within the federal constitutional sphere.[70] This law is presumptively uniform across Canada. As such, it can be described as part of the common law of Canada.

In speaking of Canadian or federal common law in this context, we are not referring to English common law, which as noted earlier is the source of various private law systems in Canada outside of Quebec. Moreover, we do not intend to draw a contrast with the civil law system of Quebec. Rather, the term federal common law is meant to describe a body of basic unwritten law that is common to the whole of Canada and extends in principle to all jurisdictions, whether these feature English common law, French civil law, or Aboriginal customary law.

The doctrine of Aboriginal rights is common law in the sense that it is not the product of statutory or constitutional provisions and does not depend on such provisions for its legal force.[71] Rather, it is based on the original rights of Aboriginal nations, as these were recognized in the custom generated by relations between these nations and incoming French and English settlers from the seventeenth century onward. This overarching body of fundamental law bridges the gap between Aboriginal groups and the general community and regulates the interaction between their legal and governmental systems, permitting them to operate harmoniously, each within its proper sphere. The doctrine is neither entirely Aboriginal nor entirely European in origin but draws upon the practices and conceptions of all parties to the relationship, as these were modified and adapted in the course of contact.

In recognizing the existence of a common law of Aboriginal rights, the contemporary Supreme Court has tacitly confirmed the views expressed in 1887 by Justice Strong of the Supreme Court in the *St. Catharines* case, where he stated:

> It thus appears, that in the United States a traditional policy, derived from colonial times, relative to the Indians and their lands has ripened into well established rules of law....Then, if this is so as regards Indian lands in the United States,...how is it possible to suppose that the law can, or rather could have been, at the date of confederation, in a state any less favorable to the Indians whose lands were situated within the dominion of the British crown, the original author of this beneficent doctrine so carefully adhered to in the United States from the days of the colonial governments? Therefore, when we consider that with

reference to Canada the uniform practice has always been to recognize the Indian title as one which could only be dealt with by surrender to the crown, I maintain that if there had been an entire absence of any written legislative act ordaining this rule as an express positive law, we ought, just as the United States courts have done, to hold that it nevertheless existed as a rule of the unwritten common law, which the courts were bound to enforce as such....[72]

There are persuasive reasons for thinking that the common law doctrine of Aboriginal rights includes the right of Aboriginal peoples to govern themselves as component units of Confederation. Although the Supreme Court of Canada has not yet ruled directly on the point, some indication of its thinking can be seen in *R. v. Sioui* (1990),[73] where Justice Lamer delivered the unanimous judgement of a full bench of nine judges. Justice Lamer quoted a passage from *Worcester* v. *Georgia* (1832),[74] in which the United States Supreme Court summarizes British attitudes to Indigenous American peoples during the mid-1700s:

> Such was the policy of Great Britain towards the Indian nations inhabiting the territory from which she excluded all other Europeans; such her claims, and such her practical exposition of the charters she had granted; *she considered them as nations capable of maintaining the relations of peace and war; of governing themselves, under her protection; and she made treaties with them, the obligation of which she acknowledged.*[75] (emphasis supplied by Justice Lamer)

Justice Lamer went on to comment that Great Britain maintained a similar policy after the fall of New France and the expansion of British territorial claims:

> The British Crown recognized that the Indians had certain ownership rights over their land, it sought to establish trade with them which would rise above the level of exploitation and give them a fair return. *It also allowed them autonomy in their internal affairs, intervening in this area as little as possible.*[76] (emphasis added)

To summarize, there are persuasive reasons for concluding that under the common law doctrine of Aboriginal rights, Aboriginal peoples have an inherent right to govern themselves within Canada. This right is inherent in the sense that it finds its ultimate origins in the communities themselves rather than in the Crown or Parliament.

The Process of Constitution Building

These brief reflections serve to indicate that the Constitution of Canada has a complex internal structure, one that bears the imprint of a wide range of historical processes and events. The process of building Confederation is not restricted to the historic pact struck in the 1860s between the French- and English-speaking representatives of Lower Canada, Upper Canada, Nova Scotia, and New Brunswick, which gave rise to the *Constitution Act, 1867* and the modern state of Canada. It incorporates the treaties and other processes whereby the Indigenous peoples of America became affiliated with the Crown and eventually entered the Confederation of Canada. It also includes the various arrangements accompanying the admission of Rupert's Land and the North-Western Territory, British Columbia, Prince Edward Island, and Newfoundland, and the special terms that governed the creation of the provinces of Manitoba, Saskatchewan and Alberta.

So, the 'compact theory' of Confederation should be understood as extending beyond the context of the 1867 Act. It is a general interpretative principle underlying the Constitution as a whole, with a special significance for Aboriginal peoples.[77] Lord Sankey's classic exposition of the doctrine is suggestive:

> Inasmuch as the Act [of 1867] embodies a compromise under which the original Provinces agreed to federate, it is important to keep in mind that the preservation of the rights of minorities was a condition on which such minorities entered into the federation, and the foundation upon which the whole structure was subsequently erected. The process of interpretation as the years go on ought not to be allowed to dim or to whittle down the provisions of the original contract upon which the federation was founded...[78]

Although these remarks are directed specifically at the position of the provinces on entering Confederation, they bear remembering when it comes to the case of Aboriginal nations.

The basic principles underlying the compact theory were articulated by the influential Quebec jurist, Justice Thomas-Jean-Jacques Loranger, in 1883.[79] He sums up the matter in a series of propositions, three of which have some relevance here:

> 1. The confederation of the British provinces was the result of a compact entered into by the provinces and the Imperial Parliament, which, in enacting the *British North America Act*, simply ratified it.

> 2. The provinces entered into the federal Union, with their corporate identity, former constitutions, and all their legislative powers, part of which they ceded to the federal Parliament, to

exercise them in their common interest and for purposes of general utility, keeping the rest which they left to be exercised by their legislatures, acting in their provincial sphere, according to their former constitutions, under certain modifications of form, established by the federal compact.

3. Far from having been conferred upon them by the federal government, the powers of the provinces not ceded to that government are the residue of their old powers, and far from having been created by it, the federal government was the result of their association and of their compact, and was created by them.

Animating these propositions is a single more fundamental principle, which may be called the principle of continuity.[80] As formulated by Loranger, it provides:

A right or a power can no more be taken away from a nation than an individual, except by a law that revokes it or by a voluntary abandonment.[81]

Although Loranger has in mind the status and rights of the provinces uniting in 1867, the implications of the principle of continuity extend far beyond that context. In particular, the principle supports the view that Aboriginal nations did not lose their inherent rights when they entered into a confederal relationship with the Crown. Rather, they retained their ancient constitutions so far as these were not inconsistent with the new relationship.

This broader understanding of the Constitution gives rise to a number of separate points. First, the process of constitution building has taken place over a very long period of time. It has ranged from such ancient arrangements as the seventeenth-century Covenant Chain, between the Five Nations and the French and English Crowns, to the relatively recent entry of Newfoundland in 1949. The federal union in 1867, in which French and English peoples joined to form the new country of Canada, was a highly significant landmark in the process of building Confederation. Nevertheless, it should be understood as part of a protracted historical evolution that, in one way or another, had already been proceeding for some time and has carried on to the present day.

Second, constitution building was a varied process. The conditions that accompanied the entry of the Micmac Nation or the Huron Nation into Confederation were different from those governing Nova Scotia, British Columbia, or Alberta. For example, the Micmac Nation carried with it the Treaty of Annapolis Royal, concluded with the British Crown in 1726, under which the Crown promised "all Marks of Favour, Protection & Friendship" to the Indians and undertook that they should "not be Molested in their Person's, Hunting, Fishing and Shooting & Planting on their planting Ground nor in any other Lawfull Occasions, By his Majestys Subjects or their Dependants nor in the Exercise of their Religion...".[82] The links between the Micmac Nation and the Crown were reaffirmed in the Treaty of Governor's Farm in 1761, where the Crown's representative promised:

> The Laws will be like a great Hedge about your Rights and properties – if any break this Hedge to hurt and injure you, the heavy weight of the Laws will fall upon them and punish their disobedience.[83]

During the same period, in 1760, the Huron Nation concluded a peace treaty with the British, which received them into the Crown's protection "upon the same terms with the Canadians, being allowed the free Exercise of their Religion, their Customs, and Liberty of trading with the English...".[84] In the view of the Supreme Court, this broad provision remains in effect today and permits members of the Huron Nation to carry on certain customary activities free of unwarranted interference.[85]

The third point is that respect for national rights has been a major structuring principle of Confederation from earliest times. This principle of continuity ensured that when a distinct national group entered Confederation it did not necessarily surrender its national character as a people or lose its distinguishing features, whether these took the form of a distinct language, religion, law, culture, educational system, or political system. In its most developed form, the principle allows certain national groups to determine the dominant legal, linguistic, cultural, or political character of an entire territorial unit within Confederation, whether this be a province or an Aboriginal territory. In more modest form, it has ensured the preservation of certain collective rights of national groups within these territorial units.

As we have already seen, the *Royal Proclamation of 1763* was a cornerstone of the principle of national continuity, in its recognition of the autonomous status of Indian nations within their territories. A second cornerstone was laid in the following decade with the enactment of the *Quebec Act* in 1774.[86] This Act amended the provisions introducing English law into Quebec and restored French law in all matters of "Property and Civil Rights."[87] As such, the *Quebec Act* confirmed that it was possible for a multiplicity of different legal systems to co-exist within the territories under the protection of the British Crown, a principle that would receive extensive application as British influence spread into Africa, India and South-East Asia.[88]

The recognition of French law in the *Quebec Act* did not impair the recognition of Aboriginal rights in the *Proclamation of 1763*. The *Quebec Act* contained a saving provision ensuring that the restoration of French law would not have harmful effects on "any Right, Title, or Possession derived under any grant, Conveyance, or otherwise howsoever, of or to any Lands within the said Province".[89] This provision preserved all existing rights to land, no matter how these rights were derived. Thus, the effect of the Act was to restore to the inhabitants of Quebec their original laws and rights, not to privilege these over the laws and rights of Aboriginal groups.[90]

In their various ways, then, the *Proclamation of 1763* and the *Quebec Act* manifest the principle of continuity, which was to receive further recognition and elaboration as the process of constitution building continued into the next century. The distinct identity of Quebec was a cornerstone of the *Constitution Act, 1867*,[91] which reversed the earlier attempt to unite Lower and Upper Canada into a single province. The phraseology of the *Quebec Act* was carried forward in a provision giving the provinces the exclusive right to make laws regarding "Property and Civil Rights in the Province."[92] The distinct character of the Quebec civil law system was reflected in a clause that allowed the Parliament of Canada to make provision for the uniformity of laws in all the federating provinces except for Quebec, thus recognizing an asymmetrical element in Confederation.[93]

The principle of continuity is further reflected in the provisions in the *Manitoba Act* of 1870 dealing with the "Indian Title" of the Métis people.[94] Of the latter, a commentator has concluded:

> The contextual background of section 31 [of the *Manitoba Act, 1870*] reveals its true nature as one of the constitutional provisions that formed part of "the basic compact of Confederation" and places it in the category of provisions that guaranteed rights to minorities in order to obtain consent for joining Confederation. For section 31, a land claims agreement was reached and was entrenched in a Confederation pact, and the rights embodied in it are affirmed by section 35 of the *Constitution Act, 1982* as one of the "treaties" that formalized relations between the Crown and the inhabitants of the Crown lands when Canada assumed jurisdiction.[95]

The final point to be made is that our constitutional law shows diversity, not only in its origins and content, but also in its legal character. At various times, it has included such instruments as treaties with Aboriginal peoples, royal proclamations, royal commissions and instructions, acts of the British Parliament, federal statutes, and orders in council. In addition to such written sources, it also incorporates a set of unwritten principles and rules, which can be described as the common law of the Constitution. Some of this law was 'entrenched', in the sense that it could not be changed by an ordinary statute passed by the federal Parliament or a provincial legislature, but only by a more complicated process involving recourse to the British Parliament. However, other parts of the Constitution were not entrenched and could be altered by ordinary statute.

According to the courts, prior to the constitutional reforms of 1982, Aboriginal treaties could be amended or overridden by federal statute, without the agreement of the Aboriginal parties. This viewpoint was consistent with British constitutional traditions, under which even such fundamental documents as *Magna Carta* could be repealed by a simple act of Parliament. However it did not correspond to Aboriginal conceptions of the treaties, which were viewed as sacred pacts, not open to unilateral repeal. As Mis-tah-wah-sis, one of the leading chiefs, stated at the negotiation of Treaty Six in 1876:

> What we speak of and do now will last as long as the sun shines and the river runs, we are looking forward to our children's children, for we are old and have but few days to live.[96]

This outlook was not based on a misunderstanding. Crown negotiators often emphasized that the treaties were foundational agreements, establishing or confirming the basic and enduring terms of the relationship between Aboriginal peoples and the Crown. We see this, for example, in the observations made by the Hon. Alexander Morris, Lieutenant-Governor of the North-West Territories, while negotiating the terms of Treaty Number Four at Fort Qu'Appelle in 1874:

> I told my friends yesterday that things changed here, that we are here to-day and that in a few years it may be we will not be here, but after us will come our children. The Queen thinks of the children yet unborn. I know that there are some red men as well as white men who think only of to-day and never think of to-morrow. The Queen has to think of what will come long after to-day. Therefore, the promises we have to make to you are not for to-day only but for to-morrow, not only for you but for your children born and unborn, and the promises we make will be carried out as long as the sun shines above and the water flows in the ocean.[97]

Unfortunately, the Crown's memory proved more fragile than that of the Aboriginal parties. The treaties were honoured by Canadian governments as much in the breach as in the observance, and, before 1982, Canadian courts upheld federal legislation imposing unilateral restrictions on treaty rights. At times, this holding was tinged with misgiving. For example, in *Regina v. Sikyea* (1964),[98] Justice Johnson of the Northwest Territories Court of Appeal commented ruefully:

> It is, I think, clear that the rights given to the Indians by their treaties as they apply to migratory birds have been taken away by this Act and its Regulations. How are we to explain this apparent breach of faith on the part of the Government, for I cannot think it can be described in any other terms? This cannot be described as a minor or insignificant curtailment of these treaty rights, for game birds have always been a most plentiful, a most reliable and a readily obtainable food in large areas of Canada. I cannot believe that the Government of Canada realized that in implementing the

Convention they were at the same time breaching the treaties that they had made with the Indians. It is much more likely that these obligations under the treaties were overlooked – a case of the left hand having forgotten what the right hand had done.[99]

Nevertheless, the judge felt bound to uphold the legislation, on the ground that there was no law preventing Parliament from overriding treaty rights.

As we will now see, this situation changed dramatically with the reform of the Constitution in 1982.

Chapter 2

A Constitutional Watershed:
The *Constitution Act, 1982*

The *Constitution Act, 1982* has the effect of constitutionally entrenching a range of special rights held by Aboriginal peoples.[100] This result flows from section 35 of the Act, which is found in a separate part following the *Canadian Charter of Rights and Freedoms.*[101] Section 35(1) provides:

> The existing aboriginal and treaty rights of the aboriginal peoples of Canada are hereby recognized and affirmed.

This deceptively simple provision is accompanied by several clauses that clarify its meaning. Subsection 2 indicates that the phrase "aboriginal peoples of Canada" includes the Indian, Inuit and Métis peoples of Canada. Subsection 3 makes it clear that land claims agreements are covered by the term treaty rights. Finally, in an important provision, subsection 4 states that Aboriginal and treaty rights are guaranteed equally to women and men.

Much of the commentary on section 35 has focused on the range and character of the rights that it guarantees. While these are, of course, important matters, another dimension of the section needs to be emphasized, namely its far-reaching structural significance. In effect, section 35 serves to confirm and entrench the status of Aboriginal peoples as original partners in Confederation. The rights guaranteed in section 35 are largely collective rights, held by groups rather than individuals. These groups are political units that became associated with the Crown at definite historical periods, whether through treaties or other less formal arrangements. Section 35 not only entrenches the particular rights of these communities, it also reaffirms and guarantees their status as distinct constitutional entities.

So, the phrase "aboriginal peoples" in section 35 does not refer to groups characterized by their racial make-up.[102] Rather, it designates historically defined political units, which often have mixed compositions and include individuals of varied racial origins. Of course, just as the people of the province of Quebec are predominantly French in extraction and those in the province of Nova Scotia predominantly British, most members of Aboriginal nations trace their lineage in whole or part to pre-contact America. However, just as people of Irish, Italian, or other origins are Quebeckers and people of Chinese or African descent are Nova Scotians, there is no reason why a person of Huron or French ancestry cannot be a full-fledged member of the Five Nations. The question of whether individuals qualify for membership in an Aboriginal group depends not on their racial origins, but on the group's rules concerning citizenship. This question, like any other question of citizenship, can turn on a variety of factors, such as parentage, continuing affiliation, self-identification, adoptive status, residence and so on. In our view, however, it cannot legitimately depend on genetic characteristics as such.[103]

The constitutional reforms of 1982 had another important effect. In completing the process by which Canada became independent of the United Kingdom, it confirmed the fact that the Canadian Crown is constitutionally distinct from the British Crown, even if for historical reasons the two offices continue to be occupied by the same person.[104] So, the Canadian Crown is no longer the symbol of British imperial authority. Moreover, it does not represent, and has never represented, only one sector of the Canadian population, such as newcomers as opposed to Indigenous peoples. Rather, the Canadian Crown is the symbol of the association of the various political units that make up Confederation, including First Peoples.

We have come full circle. The modern Canadian Crown has shed its imperial trappings and taken on a role that corresponds more closely to the vision of the Great Tree of Peace, as expressed by the Peacemaker (Deganawidah), the Huron prophet who inspired the formation of the Five Nations Confederacy:[105]

> Deganawidah's tree had four white roots that stretched to the four directions of the earth. A snow-white carpet of thistledown spread out from the base of the tree, covering the surrounding countryside and protecting the peoples who embraced the three life-affirming principles [Peace, Power, and Good Mind]. Deganawidah explained that this tree was humanity, living within the principles governing relations among human beings, and the eagle perched on top of the giant pine was humanity's lookout against enemies who would disturb the peace. He postulated that the white carpet could cover the entire earth and provide a shelter of peace and brotherhood for all mankind. His vision was a message from the Creator, bringing harmony to human existence and uniting all peoples into a single family....[106]

In the Peacemaker's vision, the Tree of Peace extended beyond the Five Nations and potentially included the whole of humanity. In a way, Canada can be seen as a partial and imperfect realization of this ideal, as a multi-national Confederation of peoples and communities united in peace and fellowship.

Self-Government as a Constitutional Right

The decision of the Supreme Court in the *Sparrow*[107] case laid down broad guidelines governing the scope and effect of section 35(1), guidelines that will no doubt be clarified by the Court over the next several decades. Thus far, it is clear that the section gives constitutional protection to a range of special rights enjoyed by Aboriginal peoples, shielding these rights from the adverse effects of legislation and other governmental acts, except where a rigorous standard of justification can be met.

As seen earlier, there are persuasive reasons for concluding that the right of self-government is one of the rights enjoyed by Aboriginal peoples under the common law doctrine of Aboriginal rights. So, the right of self-government qualifies as an Aboriginal right within the meaning of section 35(1).[108] This Aboriginal right is reinforced by treaties that protect or presuppose the internal autonomy of First Peoples.

Assuming that this threshold can be passed, the question arises whether the right of self-government can be said to be an "existing" right, as the section requires. The Supreme Court held in the Sparrow case that if a right had been completely extinguished before 1982, when section 35(1) was enacted, it could not be an "existing" right under the section.[109] However, in the Court's view, an Aboriginal or treaty right that had merely been regulated by legislation did not cease to exist, even if the right had been confined to a very narrow compass.[110] So long as the right survived in some form, however slight, it qualified as an "existing" right under the section and received constitutional protection. Moreover, section 35(1) did not 'freeze' an Aboriginal or treaty right in the form it held in 1982.[111] Legislation that limited the scope or operation of a protected right could be challenged under the section, even if the legislation was already in force in 1982.

According to the *Sparrow* case, then, the question to be decided is whether the right of self-government had been extinguished by legislation prior to 1982. It is sometimes argued that this was the effect of the *Constitution Act, 1867*. Under the standard view, the Act divided all governmental powers between the federal and provincial governments, except for a few matters expressly reserved. As the Privy Council remarked in the *Reference Appeal* (1912):

> In 1867 the desire of Canada for a definite Constitution
> embracing the entire Dominion was embodied in the *British*

> *North America Act.* Now, there can be no doubt that under this
> organic instrument the powers distributed between the
> Dominion on the one hand and the provinces on the other hand
> cover the whole area of self-government within the whole area
> of Canada. It would be subversive of the entire scheme and poli-
> cy of the Act to assume that any point of internal self-govern-
> ment was withheld from Canada.[112]

It could be maintained that this complete distribution of authority extinguished
any governmental powers held by Aboriginal peoples. Since all matters could be
dealt with by the federal government or a provincial government, no room was
left for Aboriginal jurisdiction. Moreover, section 91(24) of the Act expressly
gives the federal Parliament authority to deal with "Indians, and Lands reserved
for the Indians".

However, this argument confuses the question of the *scope* of federal and provincial powers with the question of the *exclusiveness* of those powers. As a matter of
principle, the fact that a governmental body has the power to deal with a certain
subject does not necessarily mean that it has exclusive powers, that it is the only
body competent to deal with this subject. To the contrary, it is common for two
or more governmental bodies to hold overlapping or 'concurrent' powers. Such
is the case, for example, with the federal Parliament and provincial legislatures
in certain areas. Where bodies holding concurrent powers come into conflict, it
is necessary to establish which body has priority in the area. In the absence of
conflict, however, both bodies are free to deal with the area in question. So, for
example, even if the federal government had extensive authority to deal with
Indian affairs under section 91(24) of the 1867 Act, it was not necessarily the
only body capable of dealing with these matters.

It must be remembered that the 1867 Act was not the first instrument to make a
comprehensive distribution of governmental powers in Canada. From early
times, colonial governments had been empowered to legislate for the peace,
order and good government of the colony (or some variation on this formula),
and this grant was understood to confer comprehensive authority.[113] For example, the Royal Commission to the Governor of Nova Scotia in 1749 authorized
him to constitute a council and an assembly and together with them to legislate
"for the Public peace, welfare & good government of our said province".[114] As
seen earlier, the *Royal Proclamation of 1763* contained a similar provision for
Quebec.[115] Likewise, the *Constitutional Act, 1791* gave the councils and assemblies of Upper and Lower Canada the power, together with the Crown, to make
laws "for the peace, welfare and good Government" of the provinces in question.[116] The same language is found in the *Union Act, 1840.*[117] So, the *Constitution
Act, 1867* did not materially increase the total extent of legislative powers held
by colonial governments in British North America; rather it distributed between
two orders of government the hitherto undivided powers held by each of the
federating colonies.

The fact that colonial governments exercised comprehensive authority did not mean that their powers were exclusive. To the contrary, under the standard scheme, these powers were considered to be concurrent with the powers exercised by the Imperial Parliament at Westminster. Even after 1867, the Imperial Parliament was thought to hold the power to legislate generally for the affairs of Canada and its provinces. In practice, this power was exercised with increasing rarity, as Canada gradually attained independence. In principle, however, when imperial statutes extending to Canada came into conflict with federal or provincial statutes, the imperial statutes took precedence and overruled the local laws. In point of rank, the imperial Parliament was paramount and local Canadian legislatures were subordinate.[118]

So, even if the *Constitution Act, 1867* distributed comprehensive powers between the federal and provincial governments, as the standard view maintains, it did not necessarily extinguish the governmental powers of First Peoples, any more than previous colonial constitutions had done. More likely, the effect of the 1867 Act was to restructure existing levels of authority, so that the imperial Parliament, the federal government, provincial governments, and Aboriginal communities all had, in varying degrees, overlapping powers to deal with matters affecting Aboriginal peoples. Under the standard imperial scheme, there were four orders of government, with the British Parliament at the top. Whatever the merits of this arrangement, the only point to be made here is that Aboriginal governmental powers did not disappear in 1867, any more than they had disappeared in 1791 or 1840, when earlier colonial constitutions had been granted.[119]

The survival of Aboriginal political systems is borne out by legislation enacted both before and after the 1867 Act. Consider, for example, the *Indian Lands Act*[120] passed by the Province of Canada in 1860. Section 4 provides that lands reserved for the use of any tribe or band of Indians cannot be surrendered except on this condition:

> Such release or surrender shall be assented to by the Chief, or if more than one Chief, by a majority of the Chiefs of the tribe or band of Indians, assembled at a meeting or Council of the tribe or band summoned for that purpose *according to their rules* and entitled under this Act to vote thereat, and held in the presence of an Officer duly authorized to attend such Council by the Commissioner of Crown Lands; Provided always, that no Chief or Indian shall be entitled to vote or be present at such Council, unless he habitually resides on, or near the land in question... (emphasis added)

This section presupposes that each tribe or band of Indians retains its autonomy and internal political structure, as governed by the rules of the group. The Act superimposes certain qualifications on these rules, providing, for example, that no Indian can vote in a land surrender council unless he resides on or near the land in question. Otherwise, it leaves the basic structure of Indian law and authority intact.

It might be thought that the *Constitution Act, 1867* ended this position. However, an examination of post-Confederation legislation does not support this view. The first Dominion statute to deal with Indians contains wording virtually identical to that found in the 1860 Act. The *Indian Lands Act* of 1868[121] states in section 8 that no surrender of lands reserved for the use of any tribe, band or body of Indians is valid unless assented to by the Chief or Chiefs of the group assembled "at a meeting or council of the tribe, band or body summoned for that purpose *according to their rules*...". (emphasis added) Similar wording appears in Indian legislation up until 1951.[122] Such provisions clearly assume that the internal constitutions of Aboriginal groups survived the passage of the *Constitution Act, 1867*.

Section 129 of the 1867 Act supports this conclusion. The section enunciates a principle of continuity whereby laws and powers existing before 1867 presumptively remained in force in the new federation. The text states that, except as provided elsewhere in the Act, all laws and courts existing in the various provinces at Confederation, as well as "all legal Commissions, Powers, and Authorities, and all Officers, Judicial, Administrative, and Ministerial" shall continue to operate, subject nevertheless to be repealed, abolished, or amended by the federal Parliament or the provincial legislatures, according to their powers. This language is sufficient to prevent Aboriginal governmental structures, powers, and laws from being swept away by the 1867 Act. Definite legislation to this effect would be required.

Nevertheless, it could be argued that legislation of this type was actually enacted by the federal Parliament, in the form of various statutes dealing with Indian affairs, culminating in the current *Indian Act*. Beginning in 1869, Parliament passed a series of provisions dealing specifically with the governmental powers of Indian chiefs and councils. These provisions defined the legislative powers of chiefs and councils and subordinated them to the discretion of federal officials. These powers were initially defined in a very restrictive fashion and were gradually broadened over the years.

We cannot review this legislation in detail here.[123] However the basic pattern was established by the *Indian Enfranchisement and Management Act* of 1869,[124] which provided in section 12:

> The Chief or Chiefs of any Tribe in Council may frame, subject to confirmation by the Governor in Council, rules and regulations for the following subjects, viz:
>
> 1. The care of the public health.

2. The observance of order and decorum at assemblies of the people in General Council, or on other occasions.

3. The repression of intemperance and profligacy.

4. The prevention of trespass by cattle.

5. The maintenance of roads, bridges, ditches and fences.

6. The construction of and maintaining in repair of school houses, council houses and other Indian public buildings.

7. The establishment of pounds and the appointment of pound-keepers.

This provision, and others like it, clearly purported to alter the existing governmental structures of Indian groups, attributing legislative powers to individuals and groups that may not have possessed them previously, while confining these powers to a narrow range of subjects. Nevertheless, it is important to note that such measures did not build upon completely new foundations. They took for granted the existence of Indian nations as distinct political entities and introduced or authorized changes in their internal political structures.

We see an example of this approach in the second paragraph of the section just quoted. This authorizes chiefs in council to frame regulations dealing with order and decorum in what are described as "assemblies of the people in General Council", thus envisaging the existence of assemblies constituted under the customary laws of Indian bands. Another provision in the same Act (section 10) authorizes the governor to order that chiefs should be elected by the adult male members of the group and hold office for three years, unless dismissed by the governor for bad behaviour. However, this provision is left to be implemented at the governor's discretion. Otherwise, the traditional mode of selecting chiefs continues as before.

In summary, it does not appear that federal Indian legislation purported to deprive Indian peoples of all governmental authority, even if it severely disrupted and distorted their political structures and left them with very limited powers. There are persuasive reasons to conclude that their inherent right of self-government was still in existence when the *Constitution Act, 1982* was enacted. As such, it qualifies as an "existing" right under section 35(1).[125] We have focused here on the position of Indian peoples, because their rights have been the subject of extensive regulation over the past century and a half. However, a similar approach can be taken to the governmental rights of Inuit and Métis peoples under section 35(1).

In this view, one great achievement of the *Constitution Act, 1982* was to settle the disputed question of ranking in a manner that was favourable to Aboriginal viewpoints. By entrenching Aboriginal and treaty rights in the Constitution, section 35(1) ensured that the right of self-government would henceforth enjoy a substantial degree of immunity from federal and provincial legislation, except where the legislation could be justified under a strict constitutional standard. In the remainder of this paper we will assume the existence of a right of self-government under section 35 and concentrate on exploring the implications of this viewpoint.

The Character of Aboriginal Governmental Rights

Let us consider first the nature and scope of the Aboriginal right of self-government under section 35. It follows from what we have already said that the right is *inherent* in its source, in the sense that it finds its origins within Aboriginal communities, as a residue of the powers they originally held as autonomous nations.[126] It does not stem from constitutional grant; that is, it is not a *derivative* right. The distinction between an inherent and a derivative right is not a mere matter of symbolism. It speaks to the basic issue of how Canada emerged and what it stands for. According to the 'derivative' viewpoint, Aboriginal peoples have no rights of government other than those that the written Constitution creates or that the federal and provincial governments choose to delegate. By contrast under the 'inherent' doctrine, Aboriginal peoples are the bearers of ancient and enduring powers of government that they carried with them into Confederation and retain today. Under the first theory, Aboriginal governments are newcomers on the constitutional scene, mere neophytes among governments in Canada. Under the second doctrine, Aboriginal governments provide the Constitution with its deepest and most resilient roots in the Canadian soil.[127]

The Aboriginal right of self-government is recognized by the Canadian legal system, both under the constitutional common law of Canada and under section 35. So, while the section 35 right is inherent in point of origin, as a matter of current status it is a right held in Canadian law. The implication is that, although Aboriginal peoples have the inherent legal right to govern themselves under section 35, this constitutional right is exercisable only within the framework of Confederation. Section 35 does not warrant a claim to unlimited governmental powers or to complete sovereignty, such as independent states are commonly thought to possess. Aboriginal governments are in the same position as the federal and provincial governments: their powers operate within a sphere defined by the Constitution. In short, the Aboriginal right of self-government in section 35 involves *circumscribed* rather than *unlimited* powers.

Within their sphere of jurisdiction, however, Aboriginal governments possess authority that is not subject to indiscriminate federal or provincial override. This conclusion flows from the *Sparrow* decision,[128] where Aboriginal rights and treaty rights were treated as presumptively resilient to legislative inroads, except where a high constitutional standard could be satisfied. According to this view,

Aboriginal governments are not *subordinate* to the actions of other governments; neither are they entirely *supreme*. They occupy an intermediate position. In cases of conflict between Aboriginal laws and external legislation, Aboriginal laws will generally prevail, except in cases where the external laws can be justified under the *Sparrow* standard. This viewpoint recognizes a considerable degree of Aboriginal autonomy and yet allows for the paramount operation of external legislation in matters of transcending importance.

How may the Aboriginal right of self-government in section 35(1) be implemented? Here it is helpful to distinguish between two opposing viewpoints. According to the first view, the right of self-government is merely a *potential* right, which needs to be particularized and adapted to the needs of a specific Aboriginal people before it can be implemented. The latter process requires negotiation and agreement between an Aboriginal people and the Crown or, alternatively, the invocation of arbitral procedures sanctioned by the courts. In either case, the right could not be implemented unilaterally by an Aboriginal group. By contrast, according to the second view, the right of self-government is *actual* rather than potential. As such, it can be implemented immediately to its fullest extent by unilateral Aboriginal initiatives, even in the absence of self-government agreements or court sanction.

In our view, neither of these options is entirely satisfactory. To hold, on the one hand, that the right of self-government cannot be exercised at all without the agreement of the Crown or the permission of the courts appears inconsistent with the fact that the right is inherent. On the other hand, to hold that Aboriginal peoples can unilaterally implement the right to its fullest extent seems to read too much into section 35(1). It appears likely that the true position lies somewhere between these two extremes.

Let us consider briefly a solution that attempts to strike a middle path. According to this view, the right of self-government recognized in section 35(1) should be viewed as *organic*, in a sense similar to that explained in a recent First Nations constitutional report:

> Self-government is not a machine to be turned on or off. It is an organic process, growing out of the people as a tree grows from the earth, shaped by their circumstances and responsive to their needs. Like a tree growing, it cannot be rushed or twisted to fit a particular mould.[129]

We might add that, whereas Aboriginal peoples were once like trees growing in relative isolation on an open plain, they are now more like trees in a grove, co-existing with others in a complex ecological system. So, while the ancient pine of Aboriginal governance is still rooted in the same soil, from which it draws its sustenance, it is now linked in various intricate ways with neighbouring governments.

According to the organic model, the right of self-government would include an *actual* right to exercise jurisdiction over certain core subject-matters, without the need for court sanction or agreements with the Crown. The core areas would include matters of vital concern to the life and welfare of the community that, at the same time, do not have a major impact on adjacent jurisdictions and do not rise to the level of overriding national or regional concern. The organic right of self-government also includes a *potential* right to deal with a wider range of matters that lie beyond the core area and extend to the outer periphery of potential Aboriginal jurisdiction. However, this potential right needs to be adapted to the particular needs of the Aboriginal community or communities in question, either by agreement with the Crown or perhaps by arbitral mechanisms established under judicial supervision.

Under the organic model, the right of self-government is an inherent right when it operates within both the core and the outlying areas of Aboriginal jurisdiction. In neither case is the right a delegated one. The effect of agreements with the Crown is to particularize the inherent right, not to create it. So, for example, where an Aboriginal group concludes a self-government agreement with federal and provincial authorities, the group's governmental authority is inherent throughout the full extent of its jurisdiction, in relation to matters in both the core and the periphery.

At this stage, two related questions arise: (1) what are the potential outer limits of Aboriginal jurisdiction, including both core and periphery, and (2) how does Aboriginal jurisdiction interact with the powers of the federal and provincial governments? These are complex and difficult matters, which will ultimately need to be resolved on a case-by-case basis through co-operative governmental action, as supervised by the courts. Nevertheless, one approach to the matter merits serious consideration. This holds that the subject is governed by three guiding principles.[130]

First, the potential Aboriginal sphere of authority under section 35(1), including both core and outlying areas, has roughly the same scope as the federal head of power over "Indians, and Lands reserved for the Indians" recognized in section 91(24) of the *Constitution Act, 1867*. Within this sphere, Aboriginal governments and the federal government have concurrent legislative powers; that is, they have independent but overlapping powers to legislate. This approach assumes that, in the interests of constitutional rationality and harmony, the word Indians in section 91(24) carries the same meaning as the term Aboriginal peoples in section 35; that is, it extends not only to 'Indians' in the narrow sense of the word, but also to the Inuit and Métis peoples of Canada.[131]

Second, where a conflict arises between an Aboriginal law and a federal law, and both laws are otherwise valid, Aboriginal laws will take priority, except where the federal laws meet the standard laid down in the *Sparrow* case. Under this standard, federal laws will prevail where the need for federal action can be shown to be compelling and substantial and the legislation is consistent with the Crown's basic trust responsibilities to Aboriginal peoples.[132]

Third, the interaction between Aboriginal and provincial laws is regulated by rules similar to those that govern the interaction of federal and provincial laws in this area. Prior to 1982, provincial authority in relation to Aboriginal peoples was limited by the federal head of power in section 91(24), and the courts had developed a complex set of rules to define the respective jurisdictions of the two orders of government.[133] This situation did not, of course, change in 1982. However, in this view, there was one new factor. Under section 35(1), Aboriginal governments were recognized as holding concurrent jurisdiction with the federal government over section 91(24) matters. It can be argued that the constitutional rules governing the interaction of federal and provincial laws in this area extend, with relevant adaptations, to the interaction of Aboriginal and provincial laws.[134]

What application does the *Canadian Charter of Rights and Freedoms* have with respect to Aboriginal governments? This is a complex question with important constitutional ramifications.[135] One possible answer, which merits close attention, involves two basic propositions.[136] First, the Aboriginal right of self-government as such is shielded from Charter review because it is protected by section 25 of the document, which states that the Charter shall not be interpreted so as to abrogate or derogate from any Aboriginal, treaty or other rights or freedoms held by Aboriginal peoples.[137] Second, individual members of Aboriginal groups enjoy the protection of Charter provisions in their relations with Aboriginal governments.

This approach distinguishes between the *right* of self-government proper and the *exercise* of governmental powers flowing from that right.[138] Insofar as the right of self-government is an Aboriginal right, section 25 protects it from suppression or amputation at the hands of the Charter. However, individual members of Aboriginal groups, like other Canadians, enjoy Charter rights in their relations with governments, and this protection extends to Aboriginal governments.[139] In this view, then, the Charter regulates the manner in which Aboriginal governments exercise their powers, but it does not have the effect of abrogating the right of self-government proper.

Moreover, section 35(4) contains a provision ensuring sexual equality in the exercise of the right of self-government. This states:

> Notwithstanding any other provision of this Act, the aboriginal and treaty rights referred to in subsection (1) are guaranteed equally to male and female persons.

Insofar as the right of self-government is an Aboriginal or treaty-protected right referred to in section 35(1), it is clearly covered by this guarantee.

It should be remembered that First Peoples are no strangers to the doctrines of freedom and equality that animate the Charter. Early European visitors to North America were struck by the egalitarian nature of most Aboriginal societies and the remarkable degree of personal freedom and responsibility enjoyed by their members.[140] As the French historian, Charlevoix, observed in 1744:

> Born free and independent, they have a horror of the least shadow of a despotic power, but they stray rarely from certain usages and principles founded on good sense....In this country all Humanity believes itself equally men, and in Man what they most esteem is Man. No distinction of birth, no prerogative of rank.[141]

By comparison, many European societies of the seventeenth and eighteenth centuries were highly stratified and authoritarian, with little in the way of democratic freedoms, and servitude a feature of everyday life. According to one school of thought, the example of Indigenous American societies had a significant (and underrated) impact on European political thought and contributed to the formation of the ideals that led to the American and French revolutions.[142] As the chiefs of the Iroquois Confederacy have affirmed:

> European people left our council fires and journeyed forth into the world to spread principles of justice and democracy which they learned from us and which have had profound effects upon the evolution of the Modern World.[143]

The principles that animate the *Canadian Charter of Rights and Freedoms* arguably have multiple roots, then, spreading deep into both Aboriginal and non-Aboriginal societies. To some extent at least, these principles can be viewed as the product of cultural fusion, stemming from inter-societal contacts in the villages and forests of North America, with effects that rippled outward into the salons and marketplaces of pre-revolutionary Europe. In interpreting and applying the Charter, we would do well to keep in mind the complementary ideals of freedom and responsibility that have informed Aboriginal outlooks from ancient times, ideals that have continuing relevance to Canadian society today.

To summarize, the Aboriginal right of self-government has a substantial basis in existing Canadian law, even in the absence of explicit constitutional clauses of the kind proposed in the Charlottetown Accord of 1992. The original basis for this right was the autonomous status of Aboriginal nations at the time they entered into association with the French and British Crowns. The right of Aboriginal nations to govern their own affairs was acknowledged in inter-societal practice and formed a tacit premise of many treaties. The right became part of the common law doctrine of Aboriginal rights, which emerged during the seventeenth and eighteenth centuries as a body of fundamental law governing relations between Aboriginal peoples and incoming European nations. There are persuasive grounds for concluding that the right of self-government continues to exist today as a matter of constitutional common law and qualifies as an existing Aboriginal or treaty-protected right under section 35(1) of the *Constitution Act, 1982.* The right is organic in nature and may be implemented by Aboriginal initiatives within the core areas of Aboriginal jurisdiction. However, implementation in the outlying areas of this jurisdiction likely requires agreements with other relevant orders of government.

We will now consider more closely the question of how the right of self-government under section 35(1) may be put into effect.

Implementing Self-Government

Self-government means different things to different Aboriginal groups. For some, it may mean reviving traditional governmental structures or adapting them for modern purposes. For others, it may mean creating entirely new structures or participating more actively in new or existing institutions of public government at the federal, provincial, regional or territorial levels. For certain groups, it may involve developing structures of public government that would include all the residents of a particular region or territory. For still other groups, it may mean greater control over the provision of governmental services such as education and health care. In discussing the implementation of self-government, it is important to remember that there is more than one way for Aboriginal peoples to achieve the goal of greater autonomy and control over their lives. No single pattern or model can be adequate, given the great variety of aspirations and circumstances among Aboriginal peoples.

Nevertheless, several basic principles may serve as general guidelines for the successful implementation of self-government. These are (1) group initiative and responsibility; (2) Crown responsiveness; (3) structural flexibility; and (4) fiscal stability and parity. We will say a few words about each.

To speak to the first principle, it is essential that any steps toward self-government be initiated by the Aboriginal group in question and respond to needs identified by its members. External efforts to impose self-government, however imaginative and well-meaning, run the grave risk of misreading the genuine priorities and concerns of a community and disrupting its internal dynamics. External measures intended to reduce dependency may in the long run actually increase it, precisely because they originate from outside the community. Many of the problems affecting Aboriginal communities spring from the loss of control over their affairs that they have experienced, a condition that imposed solutions will likely only worsen. It lies with each group to determine the character and timing of any moves to enhance its own autonomy. Nevertheless, it goes without saying that communities may decide to join with one another in tribal, treaty, regional or larger groupings for purposes of self-government, or to participate in public governments that represent all the residents of a certain territory.

The need for community initiative is the practical dimension of the concept that self-government is an inherent right. There is a profound truth to the saying that independence cannot be given, it can only be achieved. This means that the impetus for a move toward greater spiritual and material self-sufficiency must come from within. Not only should the structures of self-government be the product of community initiative, they should be placed under group control and remain its ultimate responsibility. That is, the group must assume stewardship over its own affairs and accept the responsibilities that this entails.

Nevertheless, Aboriginal peoples and their governments do not exist in isolation but as units within a complex federal system. So, under our second guiding principle, it is desirable that self-government be implemented with the co-operation of federal and provincial authorities, which should be ready to respond in a timely and appropriate fashion to the initiatives of Aboriginal peoples. This will require such authorities to put in place flexible mechanisms and procedures for facilitating the move to self-government. It will also necessitate some clarification of the respective roles of the federal and provincial governments in the process. As we will see, the enactment of appropriate framework legislation by the federal Parliament under section 91(24) of the *Constitution Act, 1867* may be one way to achieve these objectives.

As a third guiding principle, the procedures governing the transition to enhanced self-government should be adaptable and allow for a wide range of options. In some cases, Aboriginal communities may be ready to design and implement extensive reforms in a single step. In other cases, however, a slower, more incremental approach may be preferred, in which the most important needs identified by the group are addressed first and other less pressing matters are left for implementation at later stages, in light of experience gained. For example, in the area of child welfare, a group might decide to begin by legislating for only one phase or aspect of the matter, such as supervision orders, leaving other aspects in the hands of an external child welfare agency for the time being.

Fourth, for many Aboriginal peoples, self-government will have little authentic meaning without secure, long-term fiscal arrangements as well as increased access to lands and resources to allow for greater self-sufficiency. The abstract power of self-government is an empty vessel without the material ability to carry on the normal functions of a modern government and an adequate land and resource base to cope with current and future populations. As a result of the historical processes that accompanied colonization, many Aboriginal peoples have been deprived of their original lands and means of livelihood and confined to small areas with little economic potential. The federal and provincial governments have the responsibility to ensure that the land and resource bases of Aboriginal peoples are enhanced and, further, that sufficient financing is available to allow services to be provided at levels comparable to those in other parts of Canada.

While enacted in a different context, section 36 of the *Constitution Act, 1982* identifies the main elements of the latter responsibility. The section states that the federal and provincial governments are committed to three basic objectives, namely:

> (a) promoting equal opportunities for the well-being of Canadians;
>
> (b) furthering economic development to reduce disparity in opportunities;
>
> (c) providing essential public services of reasonable quality to all Canadians.

These objectives, although framed in the context of federal-provincial relations, seem applicable to relations between Aboriginal peoples and the federal and provincial governments.

With these principles in mind, we will now consider some of the main ways to implement the inherent right of self-government within the current constitutional framework. We will focus on three techniques: (1) group initiatives; (2) treaties and other agreements; and (3) federal legislation. These techniques do not, of course, exclude one another and may be combined in various ways. However, it is useful to discuss them separately.

Group Initiatives

Under the view considered earlier, section 35(1) of the *Constitution Act, 1982* affords Aboriginal peoples a flexible and convenient method for achieving self-government. To recapitulate our earlier discussion, it is suggested that the subject is governed by the following rules:

> (a) Under section 35(1) an Aboriginal group has the right to assume control over its own affairs within the core areas of Aboriginal jurisdiction, at its own initiative and without necessarily waiting for inter-governmental agreements. It also has the right to assume control over a broader range of subjects lying beyond the core areas, by negotiating agreements with relevant federal and provincial authorities.
>
> (b) Until an Aboriginal group assumes powers of self-government, validly enacted federal and provincial laws will continue to apply, so there is no possibility of a jurisdictional vacuum existing before an Aboriginal group decides to act.
>
> (c) Once a group has established institutions of self-government, it is free to move as gradually or rapidly as it sees fit within the core and negotiated areas of its jurisdiction by enacting laws dealing with matters currently covered by federal or provincial laws.

(d) Laws passed by an Aboriginal government will take precedence over conflicting federal laws except where the latter can be justified under the *Sparrow* test. The interaction between Aboriginal and provincial laws will be governed largely by the standard rules governing provincial and federal laws under the division of powers.

(e) However, where federal or provincial enactments do not conflict with Aboriginal laws but only supplement or reinforce them, the former enactments will continue to apply in an overlapping fashion.

(f) Where an Aboriginal government repeals a law, any federal and provincial enactments previously ousted by the law will resume their application.

In practice, then, what steps must an Aboriginal group take to implement its inherent right of self-government? We will deal here only with the central case: a group that constitutes a distinct entity and possesses its own lands, whether these be held under Aboriginal title, treaty provisions, order in council, occupation, or otherwise.[144] The case of Aboriginal groups without any form of land base is different and poses a range of complex problems that cannot be dealt with here.

The first pre-condition for the exercise of self-governmental rights is the existence of a constitution that delineates the basic structure and powers of government. This constitution may be traditional, modern, or a mixture of the two. It may build upon existing arrangements or it may represent new or revived institutions. However, in the interests of certainty, it seems desirable that the main features of the constitution should normally be embodied in a written document. This document may, of course, be supplemented by unwritten principles, as is the case with the Constitution of Canada.

The second pre-condition for the exercise of self-governmental rights is the existence of a citizenship code identifying the group's members in a reasonably definite way. This code may be an existing set of rules, an adaption of such a set, or a substantially new creation. In some cases, it may be convenient for a group to start with its existing membership and leave the door open for new categories of members to be admitted at a later stage. In other cases, the group may decide to reconstitute itself at the start, by including a broader range of people or by joining with other groups to form a new unit for governmental purposes. In all instances, it is for the group to determine how it should proceed, subject to basic norms of fairness and applicable constitutional and international standards. However, the following model may prove suitable in some situations.

Under this model, the group would begin with its current members, as established by the provisions of its membership code or legislation. Where such provisions do not exist, current membership should be determined primarily by local custom and practice. This initial group would meet to decide whether it would like to expand the existing membership, to leave it as it stands, or to postpone the matter to a future occasion. The group would also decide whether it wants to join with other groups for purposes of setting up a new governmental unit, as in a tribal or treaty council. The group should then agree on citizenship criteria and embody these criteria in a code. In some cases, the code may simply be a re-enactment of an existing code. The citizenship criteria adopted should be fair and conform with any applicable constitutional and international standards. The group should then agree on an appeal procedure for cases of disputed membership.

An Aboriginal group that has a constitution and a reasonably definite membership is in a position to exercise its right of self-government within the core areas of Aboriginal jurisdiction. If it wishes, a group may do this in an incremental way, gradually assuming control over a range of matters previously administered by other governments, in a manner and at a speed dictated by community needs and priorities.

Treaties and Agreements

In many cases, it will be preferable for Aboriginal groups to pursue the avenue of negotiation and agreement in implementing their inherent right of self-government, both in the core and peripheral areas. There are often good reasons for doing this. For example, a group with an unsettled claim to a certain territory may decide to combine land claim negotiations with negotiations regarding self-government. In other cases, a group may wish to ensure that appropriate fiscal arrangements are in place before it exercises its core governmental rights. In still other cases, the group may find it convenient to settle disputes over group membership in the context of comprehensive self-government negotiations.

Agreements between an Aboriginal group and the Crown may take a variety of forms, which have differing legal and constitutional consequences. We will consider treaties first and then discuss briefly other kinds of agreements.

From ancient times, treaties have been the preferred method for regulating relations between Aboriginal peoples and the Crown. It seems appropriate that in many instances they should form a central part of the modern process for implementing self-government. As the Bella Coola District Council stated:

> The proper way to define and establish relations between our Indian governments and the rest of Canada is not through legislation or constitutional amendments, but by a basic political agreement, a covenant or social contract. A basic compact will respect the principle of the equality of peoples. It can be an

> integral part of the Canadian Constitution while it serves as a
> constitution confederating Indian nations in Canada. But as a
> social contract it cannot be changed without the consent of both
> sides.[145]

Self-government treaties might take several forms. For example, a general treaty
could be concluded between the Crown and Aboriginal communities living in a
particular region or treaty area, or even Canada-wide. The treaty might establish
a broad framework for implementing the right of self-government, laying down
basic criteria and mechanisms for negotiation or arbitration. Alternatively, particular treaties could be concluded implementing the right on a community-by-
community basis. Such treaties would give rise to "existing treaty rights" under
section 35(1) of the *Constitution Act, 1982* and take precedence over restrictive
legislation such as the *Indian Act*. They would also be shielded from unilateral
repeal by the federal Parliament, under the principles established by the Supreme
Court in the *Sparrow* decision.

It could be argued, to the contrary, that section 35(1) applies only to treaties that
were already in existence in 1982 and not to treaties concluded subsequently.
However, it seems likely that the section will be interpreted in a broad fashion
so as to cover any treaty rights that exist from time to time from 1982 onward.
This interpretation is supported by section 35(3), which states:

> For greater certainty, in subsection (1) "treaty rights" includes
> rights that now exist by way of land claims agreements or may
> be so acquired.

The phrase "may be so acquired" suggests that the expression "existing...treaty
rights" in section 35(1) has a 'prospective' application. In other words, the section is not restricted to treaties that were in existence at the time the section was
enacted; it also covers treaties concluded later on, in the years 1989, 1995, and
so on. The phrase "for greater certainty" indicates that section 35(3) does not
amend section 35(1) but only clarifies its current meaning. So, while section
35(3) itself applies exclusively to land claims agreements, it assumes that the
phrase "existing...treaty rights" in section 35(1) is future-oriented in scope. That
is, the prospective application of section 35(1) is not the result of a narrow
exception established by section 35(3) but flows from the general terms of section 35(1) itself.

Nevertheless, legally binding treaties are not the only form that self-government
agreements may take. In some cases, for example, political accords between
Aboriginal peoples and the federal or provincial governments may have a role to
play. Such agreements would lay down broad principles guiding the actions of
the parties, even if they would not be directly enforceable in the courts. Their
purpose would be to provide an appropriate context within which Aboriginal
peoples might implement self-government in a co-operative and non-confronta-

tional fashion, without fear of governmental challenge in the courts or disruption in fiscal arrangements.

The Ontario Statement of Political Relationship, which was concluded in 1991 between the Ontario government and the First Nations of the province, provides an example of such an agreement.[146] The Statement begins by acknowledging that the First Nations exist in Ontario as distinct nations, with their governments, cultures, languages, traditions, customs and territories. It also recognizes that Ontario's relationships with First Nations are to be based on Aboriginal and treaty rights, as recognized in the *Royal Proclamation of 1763* and the *Constitution Act, 1982*. The Statement goes on to affirm that the inherent right to self-government of the First Nations flows from the Creator and from the First Nations' original occupation of the land. Ontario recognizes that under the Constitution of Canada the First Nations have the inherent right to self-government within the Canadian constitutional framework and that the relationship between Ontario and the First Nations must be based on respect for this right. The text affirms that the parties are committed to facilitating the further articulation, exercise and implementation of the inherent right to self-government by such processes as treaty-making, constitutional and legislative reform, and mutually-acceptable agreements.

A proposed Political Accord drafted at the time of the Charlottetown Accord in 1992 provides a further example of a framework agreement, one that nevertheless remains unfulfilled.[147] The document recites that the federal government, the provinces of Ontario, Manitoba, Saskatchewan, Alberta, and British Columbia, and the Métis National Council have agreed to enter into a Métis Nation Accord. It states that the Accord would commit governments to negotiate on a range of subjects pertinent to the Métis Nation, while maintaining existing expenditures on Métis and other Aboriginal peoples. Once concluded, the Accord would be legally binding and justiciable in the courts.[148] Since the demise of the Charlottetown proposals, no further action has been taken on the Accord by the governments concerned.

To sum up, it would generally be preferable for Aboriginal peoples to implement their inherent right of self-government by way of agreements with federal and provincial authorities, in the spirit of co-operative federalism, so that such important matters as jurisdiction, financing, and transitional arrangements can be handled in an orderly and amicable manner. However, in the final analysis there are persuasive reasons for thinking that in core areas Aboriginal peoples may implement their right of self-government at their own initiative, without the concurrence of federal and provincial authorities.

Federal Action

While the impetus for any move to self-government should come from Aboriginal peoples, the federal government could ease the passage to self-government by amending or supplementing restrictive legislation such as the *Indian Act*, either on a general or a selective basis. For example, it might be useful if the *Indian Act* were to be supplemented with legislation laying down an optional framework for the orderly transition to the exercise of inherent governmental powers, so long as it is clearly understood that the source of the right is inherent and not delegated. Such clauses might acknowledge the right of Aboriginal groups to opt out of certain portions of the *Indian Act* at their own initiative. The clauses might also create machinery for the negotiation of self-government agreements or treaties. These agreements might then be embodied in parallel legislation enacted by all parties, including the Aboriginal group acting under its inherent authority. Should it prove impossible for the parties to reach agreement, the Aboriginal group might always opt to implement its constitutional right through group initiatives.

Conclusion

Looking back at the long history of relations between Aboriginal peoples and the Crown, we can see that profound changes have occurred on all sides since the first treaties were concluded and the first alliances forged. Not all of these changes have been for the better, and not all of the tenets of the original relationship have been honoured. Promises have been broken and great wrongs done. Nevertheless, the time has come for tears of sorrow to be wiped away and our throats cleared of dust, and for us to speak in a frank and open fashion about our future in this land that we share, Aboriginal peoples and newcomers alike.

This paper has aimed at contributing to that exchange. We have taken as our starting point the principles underlying the original relations between Aboriginal peoples and the Crown and the recognition of those principles in the *Constitution Act, 1982*. We have drawn inspiration from the consensus evident since 1982 on the need to find ways of living together and structuring relations in an harmonious manner. In searching for the common ground for dialogue, we have attempted throughout to adhere to the principle of recognition. It is our view that each party in a relationship must recognize and respect the fundamental values, goals and institutions of the other if the relationship is to flourish. In this spirit, we have called for a broader understanding of the sources of law and authority in this country and more inclusive ways of understanding the Constitution, so as to acknowledge the important role that treaties and Aboriginal rights have played in structuring Confederation. Central to this new understanding is the recognition that Aboriginal peoples have the inherent right of self-government within Canada.

In speaking of these fundamental matters, so close to the hearts of all parties, it is easy to choose the wrong words, to fumble and make mistakes. No doubt we have made our share of errors here. However, if our imperfect efforts help to clear away old misconceptions and open new vistas on our common history, these efforts will not have been in vain.

Notes

1 The original text of the Act is found in Schedule B of the *Canada Act, 1982*, Statutes of the United Kingdom, 1982, chapter 11. Section 35 was subsequently amended by the *Constitution Amendment Proclamation, 1983*, SI/84-102, which added subsections 35(3) and 35(4). In its current form, section 35 reads:

> (1) The existing aboriginal and treaty rights of the aboriginal peoples of Canada are hereby recognized and affirmed.

> (2) In this Act, "aboriginal peoples of Canada" includes the Indian, Inuit and Métis peoples of Canada.

> (3) For greater certainty, in subsection (1) "treaty rights" includes rights that now exist by way of land claims agreements or may be so acquired.

> (4) Notwithstanding any other provision of this Act, the aboriginal and treaty rights referred to in subsection (1) are guaranteed equally to male and female persons.

2 *R. v. Sparrow*, [1990] 1 Supreme Court Reports 1075. The unanimous judgement of the Court was written jointly by Chief Justice Dickson and Justice La Forest.

3 Previous note, at p. 1105.

4 Previous note, at p. 1106. The passage quoted is found in Noel Lyon, "An Essay on Constitutional Interpretation" (1988), 26 Osgoode Hall Law Journal 95, at p. 100.

5 Previous note, at p. 1106.

6 Previous note, at p. 1108.

7 Parliament of Canada, House of Commons, *Indian Self-Government in Canada: Second Report of the Special Committee on Indian Self-Government*, (Chairman: Mr. Keith Penner), presented on October 12, 1983 and October 20, 1983 (Ottawa: Queen's Printer, 1983).

8 Previous note, at p. 43.

9 Previous note, at p. 44.

10 Previous note, at p. 44.

11 For discussion of these negotiations, see Michael Asch, *Home and Native Land: Aboriginal Rights and the Canadian Constitution* (Toronto: Methuen, 1984), pp. 26-40; William Calder, "The Provinces and Indian Self-Government in the Constitutional Forum", in J. Anthony Long and Menno Boldt, ed. *Governments in Conflict? Provinces and Indian Nations in Canada* (Toronto: University of Toronto Press, 1988), pp. 72-82; J. Edward Chamberlin, "Aboriginal Rights and the Meech Lake Accord", in Katherine E. Swinton, and Carol J. Rogerson, ed., *Competing Constitutional Visions: The Meech Lake Accord* (Toronto: Carswell, 1988), pp. 11-19; Georges Erasmus, "Twenty Years of Disappointed Hopes", in Boyce Richardson, ed., *Drumbeat: Anger and Renewal in Indian Country* (Toronto: Summerhill Press, 1989), pp. 1-42 ;

R.E. Gaffney, G.P. Gould, and A.J. Semple, *Broken Promises: The Aboriginal Constitutional Conferences* (Fredericton, N.B.: New Brunswick Association of Metis and Non-Status Indians, 1984); David C. Hawkes, *Aboriginal Peoples and Constitutional Reform: What Have We Learned?* (Kingston: Institute of Intergovernmental Relations, Queen's University, 1989); Kent McNeil, "Aboriginal Peoples and Constitutional Reform in Canada", (unpublished paper, Osgoode Hall Law School, York University, Toronto, October 23, 1992); Bryan Schwartz, *First Principles, Second Thoughts: Aboriginal Peoples, Constitutional Reform and Canadian Statecraft* (Montreal: Institute for Research on Public Policy, 1986); Norman K. Zlotkin, "The 1983 and 1984 Constitutional Conferences: Only the Beginning", [1984] 3 Canadian Native Law Reporter 3-29.

12 See First Ministers' Meeting on the Constitution, *Consensus Report on the Constitution*, Charlottetown, P.E.I., August 28, 1992, and *Draft Legal Text*, October 9, 1992.

13 This account is based largely on the following sources, which differ somewhat in their details: *Connolly* v. *Woolrich* (1867), 17 Rapports Judiciaires Revisés de la Province de Québec 75 (for other sources of this case, see note 15); *Dictionary of Canadian Biography* (Toronto: University of Toronto Press, 1967-91), Vol. VII, pp. 204-06 ("Connolly, William"), Vol. IX, pp. 149-50 ("Connolly, Suzanne").

14 National Archives of Canada, MG 29, B 15, Robert Bell Papers, "Reminiscences of Henry Connolly"; information kindly supplied by James Morrison, Legal and Historical Research, Haileybury, Ontario.

15 The trial decision is reported as *Connolly* v. *Woolrich* (1867), 17 Rapports Judiciaires Revisés de la Province de Québec 75 (Québec Superior Court); it is also reported in 11 Lower Canada Jurist 197 and Brian Slattery, ed., *Canadian Native Law Cases* (Saskatoon: University of Saskatchewan Native Law Centre, 1980), Vol. 1, 70. The decision on appeal is reported under the name *Johnstone* v. *Connolly* (1869), 17 Rapports Judiciaires Revisés de la Province de Québec 266 (Québec Queen's Bench); it is also reported in 1 Revue Légale (Old Series) 253 and Slattery, ed. *Canadian Native Law Cases*, Vol. 1, 151. The case was settled out of court before the Privy Council dealt with it; *Dictionary of Canadian Biography*, note 13, Vol. IX, p. 150.

16 The following account is based on *Connolly* v. *Woolrich*, note 15, at pp. 83-87.

17 Previous note, at pp. 83-84.

18 Reported in (1832), 6 Peters 515.

19 The original passage is found in *Worcester* v. *Georgia*, previous note, at p. 547; it is quoted in *Connolly* v. *Woolrich*, note 15, at p. 86.

20 *Connolly* v. *Woolrich*, previous note, at p. 82.

21 For other cases dealing with the issue of Aboriginal customary law, see *R.* v. *Nan-e-quis-a Ka* (1889), 1 Territories Law Reports 211 (Northwest Territories Supreme Court); *R.* v. *Bear's Shin Bone* (1899), 3 Canadian Criminal Cases 329 (Northwest Territories Supreme Court); *Re Noah Estate* (1961), 32 Dominion Law Reports (2nd series) 185 (Northwest Territories Territorial Court); *Re Adoption of Katie* (1961), 32 Dominion Law Reports (2nd series) 686 (Northwest Territories Territorial Court); *Re Beaulieu's Adoption Petition* (1969), 3 Dominion Law Reports (3rd series) 479 (Northwest Territories Territorial Court); *Re Kitchooalik and Tucktoo* (also reported as *Re Deborah*) (1972), 28 Dominion Law Reports (3rd) 483 (Northwest Territories Court of Appeal), upholding the decision of the Northwest Territories Territorial Court reported at (1972), 27 Dominion Law Reports (3rd series) 225; *Re Wah-Shee* (1975), 57 Dominion Law Reports (3d) 743 (Northwest Territories Supreme Court); *Re Tagornak Adoption Petition* [1984] 1 Canadian Native Law Reporter 185 (Northwest Territories

Supreme Court); *Michell* v. *Dennis* [1984] 2 Canadian Native Law Reporter 91 (B.C.S.C.); *Casimel* v. *Insurance Corporation of British Columbia* [1992] 1 Canadian Native Law Reporter 84 (British Columbia Supreme Court); *Delgamuukw* v. *The Queen*, British Columbia Court of Appeal, June 25, 1993, (unreported). For discussion, see Norman K. Zlotkin, "Judicial Recognition of Aboriginal Customary Law in Canada: Selected Marriage and Adoption Cases", [1984] 4 Canadian Native Law Reporter 1; Brian Slattery, "Understanding Aboriginal Rights" (1987), 66 Canadian Bar Review 727 at 738-39.

22 Revised Statutes of Canada 1985, chapter I-5.

23 Statutes of Alberta 1990, chapter M-14.3.

24 In *Re Manitoba Language Rights*, [1985] 1 Supreme Court Reports 721 at 750-52, the Supreme Court of Canada held unanimously that the rule of law was a fundamental postulate of the Canadian constitutional structure, even though it was not explicitly set out in any operative provision. The Court went on to conclude at p. 752: "In other words, in the process of Constitutional adjudication, the Court may have regard to unwritten postulates which form the very foundation of the Constitution of Canada. In the case of the *Patriation Reference...*, this unwritten postulate was the principle of federalism. In the present case it is the principle of rule of law."

25 See Jean-Gabriel Castel, *The Civil Law System of the Province of Quebec* (Toronto: Butterworths, 1962). See also the Royal Edict of 1663 creating the Conseil Souverain of New France; text in Jacques-Yvan Morin and José Woehrling, *Les Constitutions du Canada et du Quebec* (Montreal: Éditions Thémis, 1992), 591 at p. 592.

26 See W.R. Jackett, "Foundations of Canadian Law in History and Theory", in Otto E. Lang, ed., *Contemporary Problems of Public Law in Canada* (Toronto: University of Toronto Press, 1968); J.E. Cote, "The Reception of English Law" (1977), 15 Alberta Law Review 29; Peter Hogg, *Constitutional Law of Canada*, 3rd ed. (Toronto: Carswell, 1992), pp. 27-44.

27 Cited in note 2, at p. 1094.

28 Previous note, at p. 1101.

29 Quoted in Asch, *Home and Native Land*, note 11, p. 27, citing Canada, *First Ministers' Conference on Aboriginal Constitutional Matters; Unofficial and Unverified Verbatim Transcript*, March 15, 1983, Volume 1, p. 130 (with minor corrections approved by the speaker).

30 See Asch, *Home and Native Land*, note 11, p. 28, citing Canada, *First Ministers' Conference on Aboriginal Constitutional Matters; Unofficial and Unverified Verbatim Transcript*, March 15, 1983, Vol. 1, p. 134.

31 Résolution de l'Assemblée nationale du Québec, March 20, 1985. The English text is reproduced in Québec, Secrétariat aux affaires autochtones, *The Basis of the Quebec Government's Policy on Aboriginal Peoples* (Québec: Secrétariat aux affaires autochtones, 1989). The original French text is found in Québec, Secrétariat aux affaires autochtones, *Les fondements de la politique du Gouvernement du Quebec en matière autochtone* (Québec: Publications du Québec, 1988), pp. 5-6. It reads as follows: "... des ententes leur assurant l'exercice:

    a) du droit à l'autonomie au sein du Québec;
    b) du droit à leur culture, leur langue, leurs traditions;
    c) du droit de posséder et de contrôler des terres;
    d) du droit de chasser, pêcher, piéger, récolter et participer à la gestion des ressources fauniques;
    e) du droit de participer au développement économique du Québec et d'en bénéficier,..."

32 The text is found in Marc Lescarbot, *Histoire de la Nouvelle-France*, 3ème ed. (Paris: Adrian Perier, 1618), reproduced in Marc Lescarbot, *The History of New France*, ed. W.L. Grant,

3 vols. (Toronto: The Champlain Society, 1907-14), Vol. II, 490. For discussion, see Brian Slattery, *The Land Rights of Indigenous Canadian Peoples* (Doctoral Dissertation, Oxford University, 1979, reprinted by the University of Saskatchewan Native Law Centre, 1979), pp. 83-85; John D. Hurley, *Children or Brethren: Aboriginal Rights in Colonial Iroquoia* (Doctoral Dissertation, Cambridge University, 1985, reprinted by the University of Saskatchewan Native Law Centre, 1985), pp. 86-88.

33   For discussion of the interplay of economic, cultural, political, and military factors, see Denys Delâge, "L'alliance franco-amérindienne, 1660-1701" (Spring 1989) 19 Recherches Amérindiennes au Québec 3-15; Gilles Havard, *La Grande Paix de Montréal de 1701: Les voies de la diplomatie franco-amérindienne* (Montréal: Recherches amérindiennes au Québec, 1992); Bruce G. Trigger, "The French Presence in Huronia: The Structure of Franco-Huron Relations in the First Half of the Seventeenth Century" (1968), 49 Canadian Historical Review 107.

34   See the text in Clive Parry, ed., *The Consolidated Treaty Series*, (Dobbs Ferry, N.Y.: Oceana Publications, 1969-), Vol. IX, 363, reproducing the text in Léonard, *Recueil des Traitez de Paix*, V; see also, Jean Du Mont, *Corps universel diplomatique du droit des gens* (Amsterdam: Brunel, Wetstein, et. al., 1728), Vol. VI, Part III, 133. The date given in this text is incorrect; the correct date is given in the English translation found in E. B. O'Callaghan, ed., *Documents Relative to the Colonial History of the State of New York*, (Albany: Weed, Parsons & Co., 1856-61), Vol. III, 121, which seems to be based on a more complete text of the treaty. The treaty was subject to ratification by the Aboriginal parties. For discussion, see Slattery, *Land Rights*, note 32, pp. 92-94; Hurley, *Children or Brethren*, note 32, pp. 119-27.

35   See Hurley, *Children or Brethren*, note 32, pp. 119-20.

36   Denys Delâge comments that the feudal imagery used by the French here had little significance for Aboriginal peoples and was soon replaced in French discourse by imagery drawn from the patriarchal family; see "L'alliance franco-amérindienne", note 33, p. 4.

37   Cited in Cornelius J. Jaenen, "French Sovereignty and Native Nationhood during the French Regime", in J.R. Miller, ed., *Sweet Promises: A Reader on Indian-White Relations in Canada* (Toronto: University of Toronto Press, 1991), p. 32.

38   Quoted in Jaenen, previous note.

39   For various views, see Denys Delâge, "War and the French-Indian Alliance" (1991), 5:1 European Review of Native American Studies 15-20; Delâge, "L'alliance franco-amérindienne", note 33; Olive P. Dickason, "Amerindians between French and English in Nova Scotia, 1713-1763", in J.R. Miller, ed., *Sweet Promises*, note 37, pp. 45-67; W.J. Eccles, "Sovereignty-Association, 1500-1783" (1984) 65 Canadian Historical Review 475; Hurley, *Children or Brethren*, note 32; Cornelius J. Jaenen, *Friend and Foe: Aspects of French-Amerindian Cultural Contact in the Sixteenth and Seventeenth Centuries* (Toronto: McClelland and Stewart Ltd., 1976); Jaenen, "French Sovereignty", note 37; Brian Slattery, "Did France Claim Canada Upon Discovery?" in J.M. Bumsted, *Interpreting Canada's Past* (Toronto: Oxford University Press, 1986), Vol. I, pp. 2-26; Slattery, *Land Rights*, note 32, pp. 70-94.

40   As cited in note 15, at p. 82.

41   Among many works, see especially Lawrence H. Gipson, *The British Empire before the American Revolution*, 15 vols. (New York: Alfred A. Knopf, 1936-70); Hurley, *Children or Brethren*, note 32; Francis Jennings, *The Ambiguous Iroquois Empire* (New York: W.W. Norton & Co., 1984); Francis Jennings, William N. Fenton, Mary A. Druke, and David Miller, ed. *The History and Culture of Iroquois Diplomacy* (Syracuse, N.Y.: Syracuse University Press, 1985); Ronald O. MacFarlane, *Indian Relations in New England, 1620-1760: A Study of a Regulated Frontier* (PhD Dissertation, Harvard University, 1933); Slattery, "Land Rights", note 32, pp.

95-125; Jack Stagg, *Anglo-Indian Relations in North America to 1763 and an Analysis of the Royal Proclamation of 7 October 1763* (Ottawa: Department of Indian and Northern Affairs, Canada, 1981); Allen W. Trelease, *Indian Affairs in Colonial New York: The Seventeenth Century* (Ithaca, N.Y.: Cornell University Press, 1960); Paul C. Williams, *The Chain* (LL.M. Thesis, Osgoode Hall Law School, York University, Toronto, 1982).

42 See Marcel Trudel, *Histoire de la Nouvelle-France* (Montreal: Fides, 1963), Vol. I, pp. 246-49; R. Cole Harris, ed., and Geoffrey J. Matthews, cart., *Historical Atlas of Canada* (Toronto: University of Toronto Press, 1987), Vol. I, Plates 33, 46, and 47. The degree of Indian presence in the area at the time of French settlement is canvassed in the recent case of *Adams* v. *La Reine*, Quebec Court of Appeal, March 23, 1993 (unreported), *per* Beauregard and Rothman JJ.

43 Denys Delâge, "L'alliance franco-amérindienne", note 33, at p. 4, aptly comments: "Deux empires s'affrontent, Anglais et Français, de même que deux systèmes d'alliances autochtones cristallisés autour de la traite. La supériorité britannique est nette sur les plans démographique et économique, et elle se traduit par le grand nombre des colons et le bas prix des marchandises. Toutefois les Anglais ne peuvent, en matière de traite, tirer parti de leur avantage économique, et c'est précisément à cause de leur supériorité démographique, qui les place en rapport antagonique avec les premiers occupants du sol. L'inverse est vrai pour les Français dont la force repose sur l'alliance amérindienne et dont les succès dans la traite des fourrures tiennent à la fois à la petitesse de leur population et à leurs connaissances ethnographiques, acquises principalement grâce aux missionnaires, mais également grâce aux coureurs de bois."

44 See Francis Jennings, *The Invasion of America: Indians, Colonialism and the Cant of Conquest* (Chapel Hill, N.C.: University of North Carolina Press, 1975).

45 See Roy H. Akagi, *The Town Proprietors of the New England Colonies* (Philadelphia: University of Pennsylvania Press, 1924), pp. 5-30; Melville Egleston, *The Land System of the New England Colonies*, Johns Hopkins University Studies, 4th Series, XI-XII (Baltimore: 1886), pp. 6-10; MacFarlane, *Indian Relations*, note 41, pp. 180-232; Slattery, *Land Rights*, note 32, pp. 112-25.

46 There is scholarly controversy on this point. An older view maintained that the French Crown never recognized any Aboriginal proprietary rights in the soil; see Henri Brun, "Les droits des indiens sur le territoire du Québec", in *Le territoire du Quebec: Six études juridiques* (Quebec City: Presses de l'Université Laval, 1974), 33, at pp. 49-51; George F.G. Stanley, "The First Indian 'Reserves' in Canada" (1950), 4 Revue d'historie de L'Amérique Française 178, and the more qualified views in Peter A. Cumming and Neil H. Mickenberg, ed., *Native Rights in Canada*, 2nd ed. (Toronto: General Publishing, 1972), pp. 80-84. However, more recent research throws serious doubt on this conclusion; see Delâge, "L'alliance franco-amérindienne", note 33; Havard, *La Grande Paix de Montréal*, note 33; Eccles, "Sovereignty-Association", note 39; Hurley, *Children or Brethren*, note 32; Slattery, "Did France Claim Canada Upon Discovery?", note 39; Slattery, *Land Rights*, note 32, pp. 70-94. In *R.* v. *Sioui*, [1990] 1 Supreme Court Reports 1025, at pp. 1052-53, the Supreme Court of Canada favoured the latter view. Justice Lamer stated for a unanimous Court:

> I consider that...we can conclude from the historical documents that both Great Britain and France felt that the Indian nations had sufficient independence and played a large enough role in North America for it to be good policy to maintain relations with them very close to those maintained between sovereign nations.
>
> The mother countries did everything in their power to secure the alliance of each Indian nation and to encourage nations allied with the enemy to change sides. When these efforts met with success, they were incorporated in treaties of alliance or neutrality. This clearly indicates that the Indian nations were regarded in their relations with the European nations which occupied North America as independent nations.

For a recent judicial discussion of the question, which nevertheless abstains from expressing a definite opinion on the point, see *Côte'* v. *La Reine*, Quebec Court of Appeal, May 17, 1993, (unreported), *per* Baudouin J. at pp. 26-32 (typescript).

47 Text in Edmund F. Slafter, *Sir William Alexander and American Colonization* (Boston: Prince Society, 1873), pp. 136-37.

48 Text in Leonard W. Labaree, ed., *Royal Instructions to British Colonial Governors, 1670-1776*, 2 vols. (New York: D. Appleton-Century Comp., 1935), Vol. II, #673, p. 469.

49 For text, see Labaree, *Royal Instructions*, previous note.

50 Text in E. B. O'Callaghan, ed., *Documents Relative to the Colonial History of the State of New York*, 11 vols. (Albany: Weed, Parsons & Co., 1856-61) Vol. III, pp. 64-65. See discussion in Slattery, *Land Rights*, note 32, at pp. 111-12.

51 Text in William H. Whitmore, ed., *The Colonial Laws of Massachusetts* (Boston: City Council of Boston, 1889), p. 160.

52 Text in Nathanial B. Shurtleff, ed., *Records of the Governor and Company of the Massachusetts Bay in New England, 1628-1686*, 5 vols. (Boston: Press of William White, 1853-54) Vol. IV, Part II, (1661-74), at p. 213 (spelling modernized).

53 For the historical background to the *Proclamation of 1763*, see references in note 56.

54 Egremont to Amherst, 27 January 1763, "Fitch Papers", *Collections of the Connecticut Historical Society*, 31 vols. (Hartford, Conn.: Connecticut Historical Society, 1860-1967), Vol. 18, p. 224.

55 Text in William L. Saunders, ed., *The Colonial Records of North Carolina*, 10 vols. (Raleigh, N.C.: P.M. Hale, 1886-90), Vol. 6, pp. 974-76. For discussion, see especially Slattery, *Land Rights*, note 32, at p. 192 ff.

56 For discussion of the historical context and application of the *Proclamation of 1763*, see especially Clarence W. Alvord, "The Genesis of the Proclamation of 1763" (1908) 36 Michigan Pioneer and Historical Society Collections 20; Clarence W. Alvord, *The Mississippi Valley in British Politics*, 2 vols. (Cleveland: Arthur H. Clark Co., 1917); Louis DeVorsey Jr., *The Indian Boundary in the Southern Colonies, 1763-1775* (Chapel Hill, N.C.: University of North Carolina Press, 1966); Gipson, *British Empire*, note 41, Vol. IX, pp. 41-54; R.A. Humphreys, "Lord Shelburne and the Proclamation of 1763" (1934) 49 English Historical Review 241; Jack M. Sosin, *Whitehall and the Wilderness: The Middle West in British Colonial Policy, 1760-1775* (Lincoln: University of Nebraska Press, 1961); Stagg, *Anglo-Indian Relations*, note 41. For legally oriented discussions of the Proclamation and its effects, see Jacqueline Beaulieu, Christiane Cantin, and Maurice Ratelle, "La Proclamation royale de 1763: le droit refait l'histoire", (1989) 49 Revue du Barreau 317; Brun, "Les droits des indiens sur le territoire du Québec", note 46, at pp. 63-73; Cumming and Mickenberg, ed., *Native Rights in Canada*, note 46, pp. 23-30, 85-88, 167-69; Paul Dionne, "Les postulats de la Commission Dorion et le titre aborigène au Québec: vingt ans après", (1991) 51 Revue du Barreau 127; Kenneth M. Narvey, "The Royal Proclamation of 7 October 1763" (1973-74) 38 Saskatchewan Law Review 123; Slattery, *Land Rights*, cited in note 32, pp. 191-349; Brian Slattery, "The Legal Basis of Aboriginal Title", in Frank Cassidy, ed., *Aboriginal Title in British Columbia: Delgamuukw v. The Queen* (Lantzville, B.C.: Oolichan Books, 1992) at pp. 121-29.

57 *Calder* v. *Attorney-General of British Columbia* [1973] Supreme Court Reports 313, at pp. 394-95. This passage was quoted with approval by Lord Denning, M.R., in *R.* v. *Secretary of State for Foreign and Commonwealth Affairs, ex parte Indian Association of Alberta*, [1982] 2 All England Law Reports 118 at pp. 124-25, who also stated at p. 124: "To my mind the royal proclamation of 1763 was equivalent to an entrenched provision in the constitution of the colonies in North America. It was binding on the Crown 'so long as the sun rises and the river flows'".

58 The most accurate printed text of the Proclamation is given in Clarence S. Brigham, ed., *British Royal Proclamations Relating to America*, Vol. 12, Transactions and Collections of the American Antiquarian Society (Worcester, Mass.: American Antiquarian Society, 1911), pp. 212-18. We follow this text here. A less accurate version is reproduced in R.S.C. 1985, Appendix II, No. 1. The original text, entered on the Patent Roll for the regnal year 4 Geo. III, is found in the United Kingdom Public Record Office: c. 66/3693 (back of roll).

59 The other new colonies were East Florida, West Florida, and Grenada.

60 See discussion and references in Kenneth Roberts-Wray, *Commonwealth and Colonial Law* (London: Stevens & Sons, 1966), pp. 369-70.

61 Royal Instructions to Governor Murray of Quebec, December 7, 1763; text in Adam Shortt and Arthur G. Doughty, ed., *Documents Relating to the Constitutional History of Canada, 1759-1791*, 2nd ed., 2 vols. (Ottawa: King's Printer, 1918), Vol. I, 181.

62 Previous note, Article 60, at p. 199.

63 Previous note, Article 61, at p. 199.

64 Previous note, Article 62, at p. 200.

65 Quoted in Donald A. Grinde Jr. and Bruce E. Johansen, *Exemplar of Liberty: Native America and the Evolution of Democracy* (Los Angeles, Calif.: University of California American Indian Studies Center, 1991), at pp. 11-12, citing "Propositions made by the Five Nations of Indians", Albany, 20 July 1698, Indian Boxes, box 1, Manuscript Division, New York Public Library.

66 The evolution of modern legal thinking on the subject can be traced in the following commentaries (listed in chronological order): Gerard V. LaForest, *Natural Resources and Public Property under the Canadian Constitution* (Toronto: University of Toronto Press, 1969), pp. 108-33; Douglas Sanders and others, *Native Rights in Canada* (Toronto: Indian-Eskimo Association of Canada, 1970); Cumming and Mickenberg, *Native Rights in Canada*, 2nd ed., note 46; Kenneth Lysyk, "The Indian Title Question in Canada: An Appraisal in the Light of Calder", (1973) 51 Canadian Bar Review 450; Douglas Sanders, "The Nishga Case", (1973) British Columbia Studies (no. 19) 3; J.C. Smith, "The Concept of Native Title", (1974) 24 University of Toronto Law Journal 1; Brun, "Les droits des indiens sur le territoire du Québec", note 46; Slattery, *Land Rights*, note 32; Geoffrey S. Lester, *The Territorial Rights of the Inuit of the Canadian Northwest Territories: A Legal Argument* (Doctoral Thesis, Osgoode Hall Law School, York University, 1981); Leroy Littlebear, "A Concept of Native Title", (1982) 5 Can. Legal Aid Bul. (Nos. 2 & 3) 99; Brian Slattery, *Ancestral Lands, Alien Laws: Judicial Perspectives on Aboriginal Title* (Saskatoon, Sask.: University of Saskatchewan Native Law Centre, 1983); Menno Boldt and J. Anthony Long, ed., *The Quest for Justice: Aboriginal People and Aboriginal Rights* (Toronto: University of Toronto Press, 1985); René Dussault and Louis Borgeat, *Traité de droit administratif*, 2ᵉ ed. (Quebec City: Presses de l'Université Laval, 1986), Vol. II, pp. 88-109; Brian Slattery, "Understanding Aboriginal Rights", (1987) 66 Canadian Bar Review 727; Kent McNeil, *Common Law Aboriginal Title* (Oxford: Clarendon Press, 1989); Jack Woodward, *Native Law* (Toronto: Carswell, 1989); Kent McNeil, "The Temagami Indian Land Claim: Loosening the Judicial Strait-jacket", in Matt Bray and Ashley Thomson, ed., *Temagami: A Debate on Wilderness* (Toronto: Dundurn Press, 1990), 185; Brian Slattery, "First Nations and the Constitution: A Question of Trust", (1992) 71 Canadian Bar Review 261; Peter W. Hogg, *Constitutional Law of Canada*, 3rd ed. (Scarborough, Ont.: Carswell, 1992), pp.679-82.

67 See Slattery, "Understanding Aboriginal Rights", note 66, at pp. 732, 744-45.

68 See especially the following Supreme Court decisions, which discuss Aboriginal rights and their relation to treaty rights: *Calder* v. *Attorney-General of British Columbia*, note 57; *Guerin* v.

The Queen [1984] 2 Supreme Court Reports 335; *Simon* v. *The Queen*, [1985] 2 Supreme Court Reports 387; *Roberts* v. *Canada* [1989] 1 Supreme Court Reports 322; *R.* v. *Sparrow*, note 2; *R.* v. *Sioui*, note 46. The modern Supreme Court has in effect confirmed a view expressed in the nineteenth century by a majority of Supreme Court justices in *St. Catharines Milling and Lumber Company* v. *The Queen* (1887), 13 Supreme Court Reports 577, a view that was over-shadowed at the time by the ambiguous views of the British Privy Council on further appeal, as reported in (1888), 14 Appeal Cases 46. In *St. Catharines*, the Supreme Court split four-two on the question of which government, federal or provincial, took the benefit of a cession of Indian lands, with the majority (Ritchie CJ, Fournier, Henry and Taschereau JJ) favouring the provincial government and a minority (Strong and Gwynne JJ) supporting the federal government. However, on the question of the existence of Aboriginal title, the Court split in a differ-ent manner, with four judges (Ritchie, CJ, Fournier, Strong and Gwynne JJ) supporting the view that Aboriginal land rights existed in one form or another under Canadian law, and two judges (Henry and Taschereau JJ) apparently denying this; see 13 Supreme Court Reports 577, especially at pp. 599-600, 608-16, 638, 639, 643-45, 663-64. For recent judicial treat-ments of the doctrine of Aboriginal rights, see esp. the judgement of the British Columbia Court of Appeal in *Delgamuukw* v. *The Queen*, note 21, and the judgement of the High Court of Australia in *Mabo* v. *Queensland* (1992), 107 Australian Law Reports 1.

69 *Calder* v. *Attorney-General of British Columbia*, note 57, at p. 328.

70 See *Roberts*, note 68, at p. 340, where Justice Wilson identified the precise question to be resolved in the case as "whether the law of aboriginal title is federal common law". To this question she responded: "I believe that it is. In *Calder* v. *Attorney-General of British Columbia* [note 57], this Court recognized aboriginal title as a legal right derived from the Indians' his-toric occupation and possession of their tribal lands. As Dickson J...pointed out in *Guerin* [note 68], aboriginal title pre-dated colonization by the British and survived British claims of sovereignty." For discussion of this holding, see John M. Evans and Brian Slattery, "Federal Jurisdiction – Pendent Parties – Aboriginal Title and Federal Common Law – Charter Challenges – Reform Proposals: *Roberts* v. *Canada*" (1989) 68 Canadian Bar Review 817 at pp. 829-32. See also *Bisaillon* v. *Keable*, [1983] 2 Supreme Court Reports 60, where the Supreme Court of Canada held that common law rules that fall within the jurisdiction of the federal Parliament are paramount to provincial laws. Justice Beetz stated for the Court at p. 108: "...I do not see why the federal Parliament is under an obligation to codify legal rules if it wishes to ensure that they have paramountcy over provincial laws, at least when some of those legal rules fall under its exclusive jurisdiction...".

71 On this broad usage, see *Black's Law Dictionary*, 5th ed. (St. Paul, Minn.: West Publishing Co., 1979), pp. 250-51.

72 *St. Catharines Milling and Lumber Co.* v. *The Queen* (1887), 13 Supreme Court Reports 577 at pp. 612-13. See also his statement at pp. 615-16: "To summarize these arguments, which appear to me to possess great force, we find, that at the date of confederation the Indians, by the constant usage and practice of the crown, were considered to possess a certain proprietary interest in the unsurrendered lands which they occupied as hunting grounds; that this usage had either ripened into a rule of the common law as applicable to the American Colonies, or that such a rule had been derived from the law of nations and had in this way been imported into the Colonial law as applied to Indian Nations...".

73 Cited in note 46.

74 Cited in note 18.

75 Note 46, at p. 1054.

76 Previous note, at p. 1055.

77 For discussion of the classic compact theory, see, for example, Morin and Woehrling, *Les Constitutions du Canada et du Quebec*, note 25, pp. 153-64; G.F.G. Stanley, "Act or Pact? Another Look at Confederation", in Ramsay Cook, ed., *Confederation* (Toronto: University of Toronto Press, 1967), pp. 94-118. For the application of the compact theory to Aboriginal peoples, see J.E. Foster, "Indian-White Relations in the Prairie West during the Fur Trade Period – A Compact?" in Richard Price, ed., *The Spirit of the Alberta Indian Treaties* (Montreal: Institute for Research on Public Policy, 1979), pp. 181-200, and the wide-ranging discussion in James Tully, "Multirow Federalism and the Charter", in Philip Bryden, Steven Davis, and John Russell, ed., *The Charter — Ten Years After* (Toronto: University of Toronto Press, forthcoming).

78 *Re The Regulation and Control of Aeronautics in Canada*, [1932] Appeal Cases 54 at p. 70 (Privy Council).

79 Thomas-Jean-Jacques Loranger, *Lettres sur l'interprétation de la constitution fédérale; première lettre* (Quebec City: Imprimerie A. Coté et Cie., 1883), pp. 59-60; translated into English as *Letters upon the Interpretation of the Federal Constitution; First Letter* (Quebec: The Morning Chronicle, 1884), pp. 61-62. The original French text reads as follows:

> 1º. La confédération des provinces britanniques a été le résultat d'un pacte formé par les provinces et le Parlement Impérial, qui, en décrétant l'Acte de L'Amérique Britannique du Nord, n'a fait que le ratifier.

> 2º. Les provinces sont entrées dans l'union fédérale avec leur identité corporative, leurs anciennes constitutions, et tous leurs pouvoirs législatifs, dont elles ont consenti à retrancher un certain nombre qu'elles ont cédés au parlement fédéral, pour les exercer dans leur intérêt commun et dans des fins d'utilité générale, mais en conservant le reste pour en laisser l'exercice à leurs législatures, agissant dans la sphère provinciale, d'après leur ancienne constitution, sauf certaines modifications de forme établies par le pacte fédéral.

> 3º. Loin de leur avoir été conférés par le gouvernement fédéral, les pouvoirs des provinces non cédés à ce gouvernement, sont le résidu de leurs anciens pouvoirs, et loin d'avoir été créés par lui, il a été le fruit de leur association et de leurs conventions et il a été créé par elles.

For Loranger's influence, see "Loranger, Thomas-Jean-Jacques", in *Dictionary of Canadian Biography*, note 13, Vol. XI, pp. 529-31.

80 For the application of this principle in the context of property rights, see *Amodu Tijani* v. *Secretary, Southern Nigeria*, [1921] 2 Appeal Cases 399 (Privy Council), at pp. 407-10; *Oyekan* v. *Adele*, [1957] 2 All England Law Reports 785 (Privy Council), at p. 788; *Calder* v. *Attorney-General of British Columbia*, note 57, per Hall J., at pp. 401-06; *Guerin* v. *The Queen*, note 68, *per* Dickson, J., at pp. 376-79; Slattery, *Land Rights*, note 32, at pp. 49-62; Slattery, *Ancestral Lands*, note 66; McNeil, *Common Law Aboriginal Title*, note 66, esp. at pp. 161-92. For contrasting viewpoints on the doctrine of continuity, see the recent judgement of the British Columbia Court of Appeal in *Delgamuukw* v. *The Queen*, note 21, esp. *per* Wallace J. , at pars. 376-80, and *per* Lambert J., at pars. 652-62.

81 *Lettres sur l'interprétation de la constitution fédérale; première lettre*, note 79, at p. 14; translated into English as *Letters upon the Interpretation of the Federal Constitution; First Letter*, note 79, at pp. 14-15. The original French text reads: "Pas plus qu'à un particulier, un droit ni un pouvoir ne peuvent être enlevés à une nation que par une loi qui les révoque ou par un abandon volontaire".

82 The full reciprocal texts of the treaty, which are found in the British Public Record Office, are reproduced in the documentary submissions made by the defendants in the *Nova Scotia Micmac Moose Harvest Cases*, Document Books, Volume 1, pp. 159-68. For the outcome of the

cases, see [1990] 3 Canadian Native Law Reporter 87. For discussion of the status of the eighteenth-century Maritime treaties, see the decision of the Supreme Court of Canada in *Simon* v. *The Queen*, note 68.

83 Treaty of Peace signed on June 25th, 1761, reproduced in the *Moose Harvest Cases*, previous note, Document Books, Volume III, pp. 553-618; the quoted passage is found on p. 573.

84 Quoted in *R.* v. *Sioui*, note 46, at p. 1034.

85 Previous note, at pp. 1071-73.

86 Statutes of the United Kingdom, 14 George III, chapter 83.

87 Section 8 provides in part "...That all His Majesty's *Canadian* Subjects, within the Province of *Quebec*...may also hold and enjoy their Property and Possessions, together with all Customs and Usages relative thereto, and all other their Civil Rights, in as large, ample, and beneficial Manner, as if the said Proclamation, Commissions, Ordinances, and others Acts and Instruments had not been made,...and that in all Matters of Controversy, relative to Property and Civil Rights, Resort shall be had to the Laws of Canada, as the Rule for the Decision of the same...".

88 See M.B. Hooker, *Legal Pluralism: An Introduction to Colonial and Neo-Colonial Laws* (Oxford: Clarendon Press, 1975); Robert-Wray, *Commonwealth and Colonial Law*, note 60.

89 Section 3 states in full: "Provided always, and be it enacted, That nothing in this Act contained shall extend, or be construed to extend, to make void, or to vary or alter any Right, Title, or Possession, derived under any grant, Conveyance, or otherwise howsoever, of or to any Lands within the said Province, or the Provinces thereto adjoining; but that the same shall remain, and be in Force, and have Effect, as if this Act had never been made."

90 To this effect, see *St. Catharines Milling and Lumber Company* v. *The Queen*, (1887), 13 Supreme Court Reports 577, *per* Strong J. at pp. 629-35, and *per* Taschereau J. at p. 648. Justice Strong stated at pp. 631-32: "The words 'right', 'title' and 'possession' [in section 3 of the *Quebec Act*] are all applicable to the rights which the crown had conceded to the Indians by the proclamation [of 1763], and, without absolutely disregarding this 3rd section, it would be impossible to hold that these vested rights of property or possession had all been abolished and swept away by the statute. I must therefore hold, that the *Quebec Act* had no more effect in revoking the five concluding paragraphs of the proclamation of 1763 which relate to the Indians and their rights to possess and enjoy their lands until they voluntarily surrendered or ceded them to the crown, than it had in repealing it as a royal ordinance for the government of the Floridas and Granada." Justice Taschereau stated at p. 648: "From this result of my interpretation of [the Proclamation of 1763] it is unnecessary, for my determination of this case, to consider how far the sections of the proclamation to which I have alluded, have been affected by the act of 1774. I may, nevertheless, remark that any right the Indians might have previously had could not, it seems, have been affected by this act, as by its 3rd section it is specially provided and enacted that 'nothing in this act contained shall extend, or be construed to extend, to make void, or to vary, or alter, any right, title, or possession derived under any grant, conveyance, or otherwise howsoever, of or to any lands within the said Province, or the Provinces thereto adjoining'." (note omitted) This viewpoint was adopted by the Privy Council on further appeal; see *St. Catherine's Milling and Lumber Company* v. *The Queen* (1888), 14 Appeal Cases 46, where Lord Watson recited the main provisions of the *Proclamation of 1763* and concluded at p. 54: "The territory in dispute had been in Indian occupation from the date of the proclamation until 1873. During that interval of time Indian affairs have been administered successively by the Crown, by the Provincial Governments, and (since the passing of the British North America Act, 1867), by the Government of the Dominion....Whilst there have been changes in the administrative authority, there has been no change since the

year 1763 in the character of the interest which its Indian inhabitants had in the lands surrendered by the treaty. Their possession, such as it was, can only be ascribed to the general provisions made by the royal proclamation in favour of all Indian tribes then living under the
sovereignty and protection of the British Crown." See also *R. v. Lady McMaster* [1926]
Exchequer Court Reports 68, at pp. 73-74, where Maclean J., after summarizing Lord
Watson's opinion on this point in the *St. Catherine's* case, stated: "I am unable also to concur
in the defendant's contention that the Quebec Act, which enlarged the limits of the province
of Quebec, destroyed the rights of the Indians in the lands reserved under the proclamation.
This I think has been authoritatively settled." In *Attorney General for Ontario* v. *Bear Island
Foundation*, [1989] 2 Canadian Native Law Reporter 73, at p. 85, the Ontario Court of Appeal
held that Aboriginal land rights held under the *Proclamation of 1763* were not affected by the
Quebec Act but that the Proclamation's procedural requirements governing Indian land ces-
sions were repealed by the Act. For discussion, see Slattery, *Land Rights*, note 32, at p. 334;
Cumming and Mickenberg, *Native Rights in Canada*, note 46, pp. 71-72, 88-89, 107.

91   Originally passed as the *British North America Act*, 1867, Statutes of the United Kingdom, 30
     & 31 Victoria, chapter 3; it was renamed by the Schedule to the *Constitution Act, 1982*.

92   Section 92(13), *Constitution Act, 1867*.

93   Section 94 of the *Constitution Act, 1867*. The section states that any federal provision for uni-
     formity of laws shall take effect in a province only upon being adopted by the province's legis-
     lature.

94   Statutes of Canada, 1870, chapter 3. Section 31 provides in part: "And whereas, it is expedient,
     towards the extinguishment of the Indian Title to the lands in the Province, to appropriate a
     portion of such ungranted lands, to the extent of one million four hundred thousand acres
     thereof, for the benefit of the families of the half-breed residents, it is hereby enacted, that,
     under regulations to be from time to time made by the Governor General in Council, the
     Lieutenant-Governor shall select such lots or tracts in such parts of the Province as he may
     deem expedient, to the extent aforesaid, and divide the same among the children of the half-
     breed heads of families residing in the Province at the time of the said transfer to Canada...".

95   Paul L.A.H. Chartrand, *Manitoba's Metis Settlement Scheme of 1870* (Saskatoon: University of
     Saskatchewan Native Law Centre, 1991), p. 5 (footnotes omitted); see also the detailed analy-
     sis at pp. 13-14 and 110-37.

96   Hon. Alexander Morris, *The Treaties of Canada with the Indians of Manitoba and the North-West
     Territories* (Toronto: Belfords, Clarke & Co., 1880), p. 213. See discussion in Foster, "Indian-
     White Relations", note 77.

97   Morris, *Treaties of Canada*, previous note, p. 96.

98   43 Dominion Law Reports (2nd series) 150 (Northwest Territories Court of Appeal). The
     Court's decision was upheld on further appeal to the Supreme Court of Canada; see *Sikyea* v.
     The Queen (1964), 50 Dominion Law Reports (2nd series) 80.

99   Previous note, at p. 158.

100 For commentary on sections 25 and 35 of the *Constitution Act, 1982*, see W.I.C. Binnie, "The
     Sparrow Doctrine: Beginning of the End or End of the Beginning?", (1990) 15 Queen's Law
     Journal 217; Dussault and Borgeat, *Traité de droit administratif*, 2e ed., note 66, Vol. II, at
     pp. 93-95; Georges Emery, "Réflexions sur le sens et la portée au Québec des articles 25, 35,
     et 37 de la Loi constitutionelle de 1982", (1984) 25 Cahiers de Droit 145; Hogg, *Constitutional
     Law of Canada*, 3rd ed., note 66, pp. 679-95; Lyon, "An Essay on Constitutional
     Interpretation", note 4; Kenneth Lysyk, "The Rights and Freedoms of the Aboriginal Peoples
     of Canada", in Walter S. Tarnopolsky and Gerald A. Beaudoin, ed., *The Canadian Charter of*

Rights and Freedoms (Toronto: Carswell, 1982), 467; Kent McNeil, "The Constitutional Rights of the Aboriginal Peoples of Canada", (1982) 4 Supreme Court Law Review 255; Kent McNeil, "The Constitution Act, 1982, Sections 25 and 35", [1988] 1 Canadian Native Law Reporter 1; James O'Reilly, "La Loi constitutionelle de 1982, droit des autochtones", (1984) 25 Cahiers de Droit 125; William Pentney, "The Rights of the Aboriginal Peoples of Canada in the Constitution Act, 1982. Parts I and II", (1988) 22 University of British Columbia Law Review 21, 207; Douglas Sanders, "The Rights of the Aboriginal Peoples of Canada", (1983) 61 Canadian Bar Review 314; Douglas Sanders, "Pre-Existing Rights: The Aboriginal Peoples of Canada (Sections 25 and 35)", in Gerald A. Beaudoin and Ed Ratushny, ed., *The Canadian Charter of Rights and Freedoms*, 2nd ed., (Toronto: Carswell, 1989), 707; Schwartz, *First Principles*, note 11; Brian Slattery, "The Constitutional Guarantee of Aboriginal and Treaty Rights", (1982-83), 8 Queen's Law Journal 232; Brian Slattery, "The Hidden Constitution: Aboriginal Rights in Canada", (1984) 32 American Journal of Comparative Law 361; Slattery, "Understanding Aboriginal Rights", note 66; Brian Slattery, "Aboriginal Language Rights", in D. Schneiderman, ed., *Language and the State* (Cowansville, Que.: Éditions Yvon Blais, 1991), 369; Slattery, "First Nations and the Constitution", note 66; Bruce H. Wildsmith, *Aboriginal Peoples and Section 25 of the Canadian Charter of Rights and Freedoms* (Saskatoon, Sask.: University of Saskatchewan Native Law Centre, 1988).

101 For the full text, see note 1.

102 See Slattery, "First Nations and the Constitution", note 66, at pp. 273-74.

103 By contrast, some of the early legislation concerning Indians included the test of 'Indian blood' among the criteria governing membership in Indian groups; see, for example, *An Act Providing...for the Management of Indian and Ordnance Lands*, Statutes of Canada 1868, chapter 42, section 15, in Sharon H. Venne, ed., *Indian Acts and Amendments, 1868-1975* (Saskatoon, Sask.: University of Saskatchewan Native Law Centre, 1981), p. 3. It seems very doubtful that such criteria had any support in the laws of Aboriginal nations themselves.

104 See *R. v. Secretary of State for Foreign and Commonwealth Affairs*, note 57.

105 For biographical detail, see: "Dekanahwideh", *Dictionary of Canadian Biography*, note 13, vol. I, pp. 253-55.

106 Grinde and Johansen, *Exemplar of Liberty*, note 65, at p. 29. The authors describe the three life-affirming principles as follows (at pp. 28-29): "The first law of nature was that a stable mind and healthy body must be in balance so that peace between individuals and groups could occur. Secondly, Deganawidah believed that humane conduct, thought, and speech were requirements for equity and justice among peoples. Finally, he divined a society in which physical strength and civil authority would reinforce the power of the clan system."

107 Cited in note 2.

108 See our previous discussion: Canada, Royal Commission on Aboriginal Peoples, *The Right of Aboriginal Self-Government and the Constitution: A Commentary* (Ottawa: February 13, 1992). For commentary on the Aboriginal right of self-government, see Asch, *Home and Native Land*, note 11; Michael Asch, "Aboriginal Self-Government and the Construction of Canadian Constitutional Identity", (1992) 30 Alberta Law Review 465; Michael Asch and Patrick Macklem, "Aboriginal Rights and Canadian Sovereignty: An Essay on *R. v. Sparrow*", (1991) 29 Alberta Law Review 498; John J. Borrows, "A Genealogy of Law: Inherent Sovereignty and First Nations Self-Government", (1992) 30 Osgoode Hall Law Journal 291; Frank Cassidy, ed., *Aboriginal Self-Determination* (Halifax, N.S.: Institute for Research on Public Policy, 1991); Frank Cassidy and Robert L. Bish, *Indian Government: Its Meaning in Practice* (Halifax: Institute for Research on Public Policy, 1989); Diana Ginn, *Aboriginal Self-Government* (LL.M. Thesis, Osgoode Hall Law School, York University, 1987); David C. Hawkes,

Aboriginal Self-Government: What Does It Mean? (Kingston, Ont.: Institute of Intergovernmental Relations, Queen's University, 1985); Bruce W. Hodgins, John S. Milloy, and Kenneth J. Maddock, "'Aboriginal Self-Government': Another Level or Order in Canadian and Australian Federalism?", in Bruce W. Hodgins, John J. Eddy, S.J., Shelagh D. Grant, and James Struthers, ed., *Federalism in Canada and Australia: Historical Perspectives, 1920-1988* (Peterborough, Ont.: Frost Centre, Trent University, 1989), 452; Hurley, *Children or Brethren*, note 32; Thomas Isaac, "The Storm over Aboriginal Self-Government: Section 35 of the *Constitution Act, 1982* and the Redefinition of the Inherent Right of Aboriginal Self-Government", [1992] 2 Canadian Native Law Reporter 6; Darlene M. Johnston, "The Quest of the Six Nations Confederacy for Self-Determination", (1986) 44 University of Toronto Faculty of Law Review 1; Randy Kapashesit and Murray Klippenstein, "Aboriginal Group Rights and Environmental Protection", (1991) 36 McGill Law Journal 925; Leroy Little Bear, Menno Boldt, and J. Anthony Long, ed., *Pathways to Self-Determination: Canadian Indians and the Canadian State* (Toronto: University of Toronto Press, 1984); Patrick Macklem, "First Nations Self-Government and the Borders of the Canadian Legal Imagination", (1991) 36 McGill Law Journal 382; Shaun Nakatsuru, "A Constitutional Right of Indian Self-Government", (1985) 43 University of Toronto Faculty of Law Review 72; Alan Pratt, "Aboriginal Self-Government and the Crown's Fiduciary Duty: Squaring the Circle or Completing the Circle?", (1992) 2 National Journal of Constitutional Law 163; Bruce Ryder, "The Demise and Rise of the Classical Paradigm in Canadian Federalism: Promoting Autonomy for the Provinces and First Nations", (1991) 36 McGill Law Journal 308; Douglas Sanders, *Aboriginal Self-Government in the United States* (Kingston, Ont.: Institute of Intergovernmental Relations, Queen's University, 1985); Slattery, "First Nations and the Constitution", note 66; Brian Slattery, "Aboriginal Sovereignty and Imperial Claims", (1991) 29 Osgoode Hall Law Journal 681; Williams, *The Chain*, note 41; John D. Whyte, "Indian Self-Government: A Legal Analysis", in Little Bear, Boldt, and Long, *Pathways to Self-Determination*, cited above; Woodward, *Native Law*, note 66, pp. 81-83.

109 Note 2, at p. 1091.

110 The Court stated, previous note, at pp. 1097-98: "At bottom, the respondent's argument confuses regulation with extinguishment. That the right is controlled in great detail by the regulations does not mean that the right is thereby extinguished." It went on to conclude at p. 1099: "There is nothing in the *Fisheries Act* or its detailed regulations that demonstrates a clear and plain intention to extinguish the Indian aboriginal right to fish. The fact that express provision permitting the Indians to fish for food may have applied to all Indians and that for an extended period permits were discretionary and issued on an individual rather than a communal basis in no way shows a clear intention to extinguish. These permits were simply a manner of controlling the fisheries, not defining underlying rights."

111 Previous note, at pp. 1091-93.

112 [1912] A.C. 571, at p. 581. The judgement of the Court was delivered by Earl Loreburn.

113 See note 60.

114 Text in W.P.M. Kennedy, *Statutes, Treaties and Documents of the Canadian Constitution, 1713-1929*, 2nd ed. (Toronto: Oxford University Press, 1930), 6, at p. 7.

115 The Proclamation empowers the governor, council, and assembly of Quebec to make laws "for the Publick Peace, Welfare, and Good Government" of the colony; see text at note 60.

116 Statutes of the United Kingdom, 31 George III, chap. 31, section 2; text in Kennedy, *Statutes, Treaties and Documents*, note 114, p. 194.

117 Statutes of the United Kingdom, 3 & 4 Victoria, chap. 35, section 3; text in Kennedy, *Statutes, Treaties and Documents*, note 114, pp. 433-34.

118 For discussion, see Roberts-Wray, *Commonwealth and Colonial Law*, note 60, at pp. 139-40, 396-402; Brian Slattery, "The Independence of Canada", (1983) 5 Supreme Court Law Review 369, especially at pp. 384-92.

119 For a spectrum of views on the question, see the recent decision of the British Columbia Court of Appeal in *Delgamuukw* v. *The Queen*, note 21, *per* Macfarlane J., at pars. 165-75, 264, 281-83, *per* Wallace J., at pars. 480-85, 506-08, *per* Lambert J. at pars. 878, 963-84, 1011-30, and *per* Hutcheon J., at pars. 1163-73. For a broadly favourable perspective, see *R.* v. *Secretary of State*, note 57, where Lord Denning stated at p. 125: "Save for that reference in s. 91(24), the 1867 Act was silent on Indian affairs. Nothing was said about the title to property in the 'lands reserved for the Indians', nor to the revenues therefrom, nor to the rights and obligations of the Crown or the Indians thenceforward in regard thereto. But I have no doubt that all concerned regarded the royal proclamation of 1763 as still of binding force. It was an unwritten provision which went without saying. It was binding on the legislatures of the Dominion and the provinces just as if there had been included in the statute a sentence: 'The aboriginal peoples of Canada shall continue to have all their rights and freedoms as recognized by the royal proclamation of 1763.'"

120 *An Act Respecting the Management of the Indian Lands and Property*, Statutes of Canada 1860, 23 Victoria, chap. 151.

121 *An Act Providing for the Organisation of the Department of the Secretary of State of Canada, and for the Management of Indian and Ordnance Lands*, Statutes of Canada 1868, 31 Victoria, chap. 42; text in Venne, *Indian Acts*, note 103, p. 1.

122 Compare section 51 of the *Indian Act*, Revised Statutes of Canada 1927, chap. 98, with section 39 of the *Indian Act*, Statutes of Canada 1951, chap. 29. Nevertheless, the *Indian Act* of 1951 continues to allow for bands with councils chosen "according to the custom of the band"; see section 2(1)(c)(ii). A similar provision appears in the current *Indian Act*; see Revised Statutes of Canada 1985, Chap. I-5, section 2(1), "council of the band", par. (b).

123 For discussion, see Richard H. Bartlett, *The Indian Act of Canada*, 2nd ed. (Saskatoon, Sask.: University of Saskatchewan Native Law Centre, 1988).

124 *An Act for the Gradual Enfranchisement of Indians, the Better Management of Indian Affairs, and to Extend the Provisions of the Act, 31st Victoria, Chapter 42*; Statutes of Canada 1869, 32-33 Victoria, chapter 6; in Venne, *Indian Acts*, note 103, p. 11 at p. 13.

125 This viewpoint has interesting parallels with the argument accepted by the Supreme Court of Canada in *Donahoe* v. *The Canadian Broadcasting Corporation*, Supreme Court of Canada, January 21, 1993, (unreported). McLachlin J. held for the majority that certain inherent constitutional rights that existed under English common law were imported into Canada when legislative assemblies were founded here. These rights were implicitly constitutionalized by a general reference in the preamble to the *Constitution Act, 1867*. Although not specifically referred to in section 52 of the *Constitution Act, 1982*, these common law rights form part of the Constitution of Canada, which under section 52 is the supreme law of Canada.

126 See our earlier discussion: Canada, Royal Commission on Aboriginal Peoples, *The Right of Aboriginal Self-Government and the Constitution: A Commentary* (Ottawa: February 13, 1992), pp. 16-23.

127 We repeat here, in an adapted form, views expressed in our Commentary, *The Right of Aboriginal Self-Government and the Constitution*, previous note, at p. 18.

128 Note 2.

129 Rosie Mosquito and Konrad Sioui, *To the Source: First Nations Circle on the Constitution. Commissioners' Report* (Ottawa: Assembly of First Nations, 1992), p. 21.

130 For a parallel approach, see Slattery, "First Nations and the Constitution", note 66, at pp. 282-87.

131 In *Re Term "Indians"*, [1939] Supreme Court Reports 104, the Supreme Court of Canada ruled that section 91(24) applied to the Inuit (or 'Eskimo') peoples. The Supreme Court has not yet decided whether the section also covers the Métis people. A leading constitutional authority, Professor Peter Hogg, offers the view that the Métis are probably included within the section; see Hogg, *Constitutional Law of Canada*, 3rd ed., note 66, pp. 665-66. For background and discussion, see Catherine Bell, "Who Are the Métis People in Section 35(2)?", (1991) 29 Alberta Law Review 351; Clem Chartier, "'Indian': An Analysis of the Term as Used in Section 91(24) of the British North America Act, 1867", (1978-79) 43 Saskatchewan Law Review 37; Paul L.A.H. Chartrand, "Aboriginal Rights: The Dispossession of the Métis", (1991) 29 Osgoode Hall Law Journal 457; Chartrand, *Manitoba's Métis Settlement Scheme*, note 95; Richard I. Hardy, "Metis Rights in the Mackenzie River District of the Northwest Territories", [1980] 1 Canadian Native Law Reporter 1; Cumming and Mickenberg, *Native Rights in Canada*, note 46, pp. 6-9, 200-04; William F. Pentney, *The Aboriginal Rights Provisions in the Constitution Act, 1982* (Saskatoon, Sask.: University of Saskatchewan Native Law Centre, 1987), chap.4; Schwartz, *First Principles, Second Thoughts*, note 11, pp. 213-47; Woodward, *Native Law*, note 66, pp. 53-59.

132 See *R. v. Sparrow*, note 2, at pp. 1113-14. The Supreme Court held that the proposed standards of "reasonableness" and "in the public interest" were not sufficiently stringent; see pp. 1113, 1118-1119.

133 For discussion of these rules, see G.-A. Beaudoin, *La Constitution du Canada* (Montreal: Wilson & Lafleur, 1990), chap. 15; Hogg, *Constitutional Law of Canada*, 3rd ed., note 66, pp. 664-79; Patricia Hughes, "Indians and Lands Reserved for the Indians: Off-Limits to the Provinces?", (1983) 21 Osgoode Hall Law Journal 82; Kenneth M. Lysyk, "The Unique Constitutional Position of the Canadian Indian", (1967) 45 Canadian Bar Review 513; Kenneth M. Lysyk, "Constitutional Developments relating to Indians and Indian Lands: An Overview", in *The Constitution and the Future of Canada, Special Lectures of the Law Society of Upper Canada* (Toronto: Richard de Boo Ltd., 1978), 201; Micheline Patenaude, *Le droit provincial et les terres indiennes* (Montreal: Éditions Yvon Blais, 1986), chap. II; Douglas Sanders, "Prior Claims: Aboriginal People in the Constitution of Canada", in Stanley M. Beck and Ivan Bernier, ed., *Canada and the New Constitution* (Montreal: Institute for Research on Public Policy, 1983), Vol. I, p. 225; Slattery, "Understanding Aboriginal Rights", note 66, pp. 774-81; Woodward, *Native Law*, note 66, pp. 87-131.

134 See discussion in Slattery, "First Nations and the Constitution", note 66, pp. 283-86.

135 For discussion of the question of cultural perspective, see Mary Ellen Turpel, "Aboriginal Peoples and the Canadian *Charter*: Interpretive Monopolies, Cultural Differences", (1989-90) 6 Canadian Human Rights Yearbook 3.

136 Compare Slattery, "First Nations and the Constitution", note 66, at pp. 286-87.

137 Section 25 provides in part: "The guarantee in this Charter of certain rights and freedoms shall not be construed so as to abrogate or derogate from any aboriginal, treaty or other rights or freedoms that pertain to the aboriginal peoples of Canada...". For commentary on the section, see works cited in note 100.

138 For the distinction between the Charter's effects on the existence of a constitutional power and the exercise of that power, see *Re: An Act to Amend the Education Act*, [1987] 1 Supreme Court Reports 1148, *per* Estey, J. at pp. 1206-07; *Re Provincial Electoral Boundaries (Sask.)*, [1991] 2 Supreme Court Reports 158, *per* McLachlin J. at p. 179; *Donahoe* v. *Canadian Broadcasting Corp.*, note 125, *per* McLachlin J. at pp. 30-34 (typescript), *per* Cory J. at pp. 8-10 (typescript).

139   While Aboriginal governments are not specifically mentioned in section 32(1) of the Charter, which lists governmental authorities to which the Charter applies, this list does not seem to be comprehensive. In the case of *R.W.D.S.U.* v. *Dolphin Delivery Ltd.* [1986] 2 Supreme Court Reports 573, the Supreme Court of Canada held that the Charter does not apply in litigation between private parties and that section 32 was conclusive on this point; see McIntyre, J. at p. 597. Justice McIntyre went on to state at p. 598: "It is my view that s. 32 of the *Charter* specifies the actors to whom the *Charter* will apply. They are the legislative, executive and administrative branches of government." This holding suggests that the purpose of section 32 is to draw the dividing line between private and governmental actors, rather than to list in a comprehensive fashion the governmental bodies to which the Charter applies.

140   There is a large literature on the subject. Among recent works, see especially William Brandon, *New Worlds for Old: Reports from the New World and Their Effect on the Development of Social Thought in Europe, 1500-1800* (Athens, Ohio: Ohio University Press, 1986); Denys Delâge, "L'influence des Amérindiens sur les Canadiens et les Français au temps de la Nouvelle-France", (1992) 2 Lekton (No. 2) 103, esp. at pp. 163-91.

141   P.-F.-X. Charlevoix, *Histoire et description générale de la Nouvelle France.* 3 vols. (Paris: Ganeau 1744), Vol. 3, at pages 341-42; quoted in Brandon, *New Worlds for Old*, previous note, at p. 106. On the cultivation of the ideal of autonomous responsibility among the Iroquois, see Anthony F.C. Wallace, *The Death and Rebirth of the Seneca* (New York: Vintage Books, 1972), pp. 34-39.

142   The thesis is argued in Grinde and Johansen, *Exemplar of Liberty: Native America and the Evolution of Democracy*, note 65. For more modulated assessments, see Brandon, *New Worlds for Old*, note 140, and Delâge, "L'influence des Amérindiens", note 140.

143   "Haudenosaunee Statement to the World", Akwesasne Notes 11 (May 1979): 7; quoted in Grinde and Johansen, *Exemplar of Liberty*, note 65, at p. 235.

144   We have in mind here the widest possible category of lands held by Aboriginal peoples, ranging from 'reserve' or 'settlement' lands to lands held by occupation or historical title.

145   Quoted in *Indian Self-Government in Canada* (the Penner Report), note 7, at p.45.

146   The agreement was dated August 6, 1991. The text provides in section 5 that the statement expresses the political commitment of the parties and is not intended to be a treaty or to affect the rights or obligations of the parties.

147   See the document entitled "Political Accords: The Multilateral Meetings on the Constitution", dated August 28, 1992, at p. 4. The document is prefaced with this explanatory note: "This companion document to the Consensus Report [The Consensus Report on the Constitution, Charlottetown, August 28, 1992, Final Text] describes the elements of a political accord or accords that will accompany the constitutional amendments, as well as intergovernmental agreements that may be negotiated pursuant to these amendments."

148   The text speaks of "a legally binding, justiciable and enforceable accord...".

For further information:
Royal Commission on Aboriginal Peoples
P.O. Box 1993, Station B
Ottawa, Ontario
K1P 1B2

Telephone: (613) 943-2075
Facsimile: (613) 943-0304

Toll-free:
1-800-363-8235 (English, French, Chipewyan)
1-800-387-2148 (Cree, Inuktitut, Ojibwa)